Meditations
for
Spiritual Misfits

Robert Badra
1983

Cover design and illustrations by Judith Lynn
Printed in the United States of America
Published by: JCL House
               P.O. Box 1821
               East Lansing, MI 48823

"Philosophy is just another form of sightseeing."
Bertrand Russell

To My Fellow Travelers

Razouk, My Father, who never returned to Aleppo, Syria —
The Carpenter Who Became A Superior Mechanic;
Anna, My Mother, who never returned to Lebanon —
Who Understands Better Than Most Philosophers;
Kristen, My Companion, Who Endured More Than I Will
Ever Tell So That I Would Have My Day In The
Outback.

Forward

Actually, **Meditations for Spiritual Misfits** began quite brashly as a teacher's intellectual search for happiness in paradise. On a visit to the South Pacific, from Hawaii to Fiji, New Zealand, Australia and Tahiti, I had hoped to learn something about happiness in places where so many westerners idealize happiness to be: in paradise. I was soon to abandon my pre-determined set of objectives. What I learned about happiness went beyond happiness. What I learned surprised me. These meditations are an expression of that surprise.

In many ways we are all spiritual misfits: those of us who don't feel comfortable with institutional spirituality and those of us who do. As always, the problem rests not with God but with ourselves. I question whether there are any non-believers. There are only seekers, and to somebody my seeking does not fit his or her idea of seeking. To somebody, I am a non-believer. I am not. I cannot be. As was driven home to me in the short while I allowed myself to spend near the sacred places of the Australian aborigines, there are no aborigines. Only people. People with a spiritual dimension in their lives whether they know it or not. Perhaps we are none of us misfits after all. We are all simply struck by wonder. And that wonder may finally lead us all to love. Until then, we are misfits to somebody.

How may we move from misfits struck by wonder to love? It might help to periodically dare to let go of our institutional moorings enough to sense the dizzy and awesome heights of spirituality just outside the reach of creeds. My experience in the South Pacific amounted to a spiritual high; a spiritual high that I was able to bring back to my institutional mooring, Catholicism, but with what a difference! Blinders down, what an ambient faith can be ours, a faith that can sense the very touch of God in other ancient faiths, especially in the 40,000 year old faith of the Australian aborigine. What fine gifts of wonder and mystery we can bring to our own vision of faith! Truly, God lives beyond creeds. God lives within creeds. The creeds have to figure that one out. I acknowledge that in these reflections I am feebly reaching out to a reality beyond myself, and within myself, and beyond all selfhood, whatever that means. It must remain that way until I move beyond creeds to God. In God's good time! You see, I like it here very much, pain and joy together. I can wait to have the Grand Mystery unraveled for me.

Beyond creeds, God must surely know what it means not to fit. We are in very good company.

Robert Badra
Kalamazoo, January, 1983

A Note on Reading These Reflections

*Relax. Take it as it comes. Not too
seriously. Not too lightly. Like an
ice cream soda. Or a fine wine. Savour
slowly. Not to think so much as to
wonder. And to wonder back. These
are my risks at expressing Mystery.
Find your words too. The Mystery
loves a good conversation. By the
way, there are so many expressions
to that Mystery. When I begin certain
words with Large Letters, I only intend
to personify Mystery's many expressions
to help us identify and see Mystery's
reflections in the World we know. And
in ourselves. Sip slowly. Relax.*

The Setting

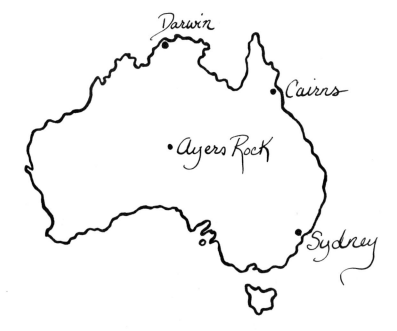

Darwin

Cairns

Ayers Rock

Sydney

Australia

The Setting: **Central** **Australia**	This is an ancient land where dry rivers flow. Sandy, their crimson tides must blow. Tongue lashed by the sun, the bushlands lie dry; hungering for water. Blue is the sky.
The Place: **Ayers Rock**	Rough hewn the stones that shine in the sun, boulders all broken, mountains each one. Shadows at play through crevices go; thus might the stories of spirits grow.
The People: **Loritdja** **Aboriginals**	Worshipful eyes connect with this sight, praying for rain to fall in the night. Lo! Every drop falls thunderously soft! Breaking the dust: response from Aloft!
The Outcome: **An Enduring** **Ritual**	Spirits that listen! Stories begin! Stories of Eden, stories of sin. People who stand in awe of each tale, conjure a priest-hood; heaven and hell.
An Enduring **People**	Thus did a people astrewn on this land, form for themselves a life in the sand. Mystery did render their arid lives green. Dreamtime began when shadows were seen!

I
Children of the Dreamtime

Ayers Rock

**Inspired At
Ayers Rock:
Movements In
The Commotion
Of Creation**

**The First
Movement:
The Moment
Before
The Moment**

In the beginning, in that strung-out timelessness preceding the invention of the first Chinese kite, there lived a lone and breathtaking Being who at once was filled with the motion of the sea before the sea was made, and who at once was as empty as a pelican's beak soon after the rising of the moon.

Since there was as yet neither moon nor sea, the Being not yet having dreamed dreams that come true, and since it was difficult to take pride in being all-knowing since as yet there was only Nothing to know and Nothing not being enough, the lone and breathtaking Being dreamed a gentle Breeze to be born, a second breath.

The second Breath took the Being, and the divine nostrils were seized by such a salty Urge that the divine tongue became parched with Thirst, a condition never known before, and such a solitary Thirst was this, that the breathtaking Being exhaled from that Breath a tertiary being, Trust, who assured the divine Being that something called Wetness would quench the divine slack soon enough.

A loud and echoing moan was followed by Rain and the Being was immediately spoiled by Trust since the fulfillment of this need produced the need to quench other thirsts that had never been known before: the thirst for Sensations, the thirst for Perceptions, the thirst for Wonder, the Thirst for Quests, the thirst for Responses; a taste for Doubt, a taste for Surprise, a taste for Fear, a taste for Mystery, a taste for Being.

Thus was the Being's eternal Rest jarred and that Being's dreamlessness broken, and the Being began to dream incredible dreams, such as the dream of communing with other beings, and with each incredible dream an Urge arose higher and higher, until that Urge became a Fire that cannot be snuffed out, the Urge to make incredible dreams come true.

Thus was Fire created, deep within the bowels of the Being's first dream.

Suddenly, sensitive to the presence of new beings, beings other than, being no longer alone but breathtaking still, ignorant of the power of Power, and with simultaneous expressions of irresistible contrapositions constantly emerging, the Being experienced omnipresence for the first Time, and Time was duly impressed, forever.

The Being was impressed too.

Now, knowing need, the Being was truly omniscient; and Filling the Breeze, the Flame and Time, truly omnipresent, the Urge grew and grew to fill other beings, to do other dream-fulfilling deeds, there being so much Time and so many dreams rushing for fulfillment, and such a Rush!

From such a Rush flowed forth riots of cacophonous off-springing, intense sparks surrounded by cocoons of shyness, each shy spark eventually piercing its translucent bubble, each joining the others in an endless symphonic overture of gregarious daring, bursting to meet and touch and know what else is new.

Music came to pass the Time. The Being wanted to Dance. But for now, too shy, listened, and waited.

The Being's shyness is understandable, since up until now self-knowledge was painfully difficult, there being no others to reflect on oneself; now that there were others, Insecurity prevailed, for how should the Other receive the others, and how should the others receive the Other in this precedent-shattering aborning?

Thus did the Being experience both Delight and Anguish, a normal post-partum.

So was Relationship begotten: an intensely satisfying and challenging new creation. From Relationship would come at least one child: Self-Knowledge. The Being would come to self-knowledge through knowing these others, to a degree not possible Before the Beginning.

The Second Movement: The Moment

All the promises of broken dreams that plague the inexperienced filled that moment. It was a moment of Torment both for the Being and for the Great Rush. The Being knew Complaint, the Complaint of Rapid Change. The Rush of such Rapid Change became a severe demand on the Being.

This the Being also knew: that there would always be the Rush, that constant state of inconsistency that dazzles and frequently overwhelms both aware and dull beings alike.

With Time came Fear, Fear that crawls like a million spiders in the bog of the brain. This, mind you, was but the stubble of Creation, unnerved and not knowing what to make of itself, fearing most of all the bright smile of Care, the eternal harbinger of Great Responsibility.

It was Curiosity, blessed Curiosity that prevented the Being from fleeing both the Dream and the Consequences of that Dream, each bearing heavily upon the Being, moving the Being to be more involved, and the Being made bold and received Greater Involvement with some Reluctance, driven on as the Being was by this marvelous and blessed Curiosity, which is the ever throbbing wonder of what would happen next.

For this reason, the Being developed an infinite Patience which kept destruction of the Dream and of the Dream's Children far from the Being's mind since the Being was now intent to know what would come next, no matter what.

Not too surprisingly, and adding infinitely to the Spice of Creation, each Child of the Dream became a speck of Determination, each intent on establishing Dreams of its own, a daring desire. But some ''specks'' rather created a ''hell'' of sorts, a place of torments that so often goes with daring dreams, but the Being was not too dismayed. Watching with interest what became the Being's Loyal Opposition, which gave the Being much laughter, each emboldened speck carried its own light right into the Being's face, as though hardly aware of the Greater Light, the totally penetrating and totally penetrable One.

Such power gave the Being heady sensations of Clarity and Delight. In fact, as the Being's power manifested itself more and more in the shape of beings still-a-coming, the Being's self-control and control over the others gradually diminished until neither the Other nor the others could tell who or what generated whom or whatever.

To complete the agonizing Delight, the Being felt feelings of feminine fusion, and infinite Motherhood joined infinite Fatherhood, until Infinity and Time were united in Marriage, the primary purpose of which would be the continued passing on of the gift of Being called Life.

From whence comes Immortality, something that the inventors of the Chinese kite knew all along.

The Third Movement: The Moment After The Moment

Imagine the Being's consternation at seeing Everything for the first time. The best way to see this is to imagine Nothing. But you can't imagine Nothing. Not really. Nothing is far beyond mortal conception. Nothing belongs to the realm of God.

Strange as it may seem to us, the condition of not-being-at-all is a sensation we cannot conjure, most likely because none of us can remember what it was like to be the Only-Being-At-All.

Before there were others, the Other was breathtaking, but lone.

The Being was lonely.

From Loneliness all creation sprang.

II
Ritual Man: Ritual Woman

Olga Mountains

Dreamtime's Children

We are all Children of the Dreamtime, the time when Human Life on Earth began. All human societies have commemorated that mystical event, each in its own way. The society that listens only to its own version of Creation and rejects other versions tends to do battle on behalf of its own version against all the rest. This is the dogmatic sense of the Dreamtime, and insofar as it lacks a sense of humor, such a society takes itself too seriously and would find it difficult to live with other societies in peace. This is an unnecessary battle, for there was only one Dreamtime. Thus the need to listen with a sense of humor to our own vision and recognize in that other society's vision, our own.

To Touch Life's Mystery

Every man or woman who ever lived, no matter how "primitive" their society, held in common with me a lofty aspiration. I aspire to join my own life's meaning with the meaning of the whole of life. I want to touch Life's mystery through my own mystery. By my choice do I so aspire. My life's meaning is not tied to purpose. Since Life is it's own meaning, I can submit to that Larger Mystery as I submit to the air I breath. I can have all the little or big purposes I want in my little life. Unless I submit to that Larger Mystery, I will still be searching for my life's meaning. But if I allow myself to leap beyond purposes, every moment of my life will grace my mind and heart in the deepest silences of Love. The next time someone asks me if my life has meaning, I will not use words to prove or defend anything. My smile will say it all.

Ritual Is A Greeting

Life is, after all, that mystery which fills us and in which we move and have our being. Ritual helps us to be at ease with the Deniable-Undeniable, the throat clutcher. To enhance our inner-most tendency to fear and to wonder, we turn to ritual. At first, we greet mystery in her own tongue, silently. Mystery provokes. We don't know what to say to her. It is informal ritual with which we so greet her silence. It is my ritual. My way of feeling at home with her. I want to be on good terms with her. I can only be so comfortable with her on her terms. Yet this informal ritual, so unique to me, craves a common expression. I am a social being as well as an individual being. It is for this reason that many of us turn to a formal ritual, as provided by institutional religions, to greet mystery. Both rituals can be valid expressions if we keep in mind that we walk on sacred ground. Mystery is still mystery, no matter how formally we greet her. Those of us who attend formal rituals and complain that they do not speak to us have forgotten two things: we take our personal, private, unique and informal ritual with us, for our informal ritual gives life to the formal; and words always fail.

Mystery Loves Company

Many of us claim to satisfy our need for "worship" in natural settings. Naturally. Mystery is natural. This kind of "worship" is an informal ritual. The formal ritual, as exemplified by church services, is empty if we do not take our "walks in the garden" with us to that ritual. Fifty-thousand people may gather to pray. But if they have not greeted the mystery in intimate, lonely moments of the heart, inspired by gardens, stars, lovers, or tragedy, the formal ritual will fall flat, or be taken too seriously. To go fishing on a Sunday morning may often be a better choice. Mystery enjoys life. It's no fun to take ritual too seriously.

Mystery Provokes

Life is, after all, a mystery. To surround mystery with ritual is to greet her in her own tongue. Ritual helps us to be at ease with the Deniable-Undeniable. Mystery provokes. We want to be on good terms with her. We want to be at home with her. But we must never forget that it is her home, and we can be at ease with her only on her terms.

Mystery Is Natural

Ritual is our response to the largely Unknown. No matter how much I think I know about this mystery called Life, I don't know what I don't know. The enormous remainder of what is left when I subtract what I know from who-knows-what-is-left-unknown demands a ritual. It is a "gut" thing. It is a "gut" thing that leads to awe. The most we can do in a ritual is to send greetings of recognition to that mystery. In exchange, the mystery rewards us with a glow that comes not from some distant star but from within our own ability to be aware. To greet the presence of mystery within us is to glow. When we are radiant, mystery glows from within us. When we experience dullness, it is but the momentary absence of mystery. When dullness seems permanent, this is hell. Mystery is irreplaceable. We either glow in her presence or we are bored in her absence. But she is never absent. We only refuse to greet her. Ritual, then, is natural. Because mystery is natural. And whether alone in the fields or with others in a formal rite, whenever mystery is truly celebrated, even when words are used, such words will not speak of what is known, but of what is not known. Not even the finest expression of formal ritual can surpass a smile!

Where Is Paradise

I smiled when I stood before Ayers Rock which the natives call Uluru: Ritual Stone.

I made room for what was already in me. I was not a stranger in paradise. Paradise had been a stranger, ignored and unrecognized, in me.

A Happy Wordless Moment

Clearly this was a happy moment. While I felt the need to express what I was experiencing in words, I knew the futility. Words are but bubbles on the surface of much deeper realities. Yet words must try, humbly, as with the telling of love, falling short, yet not missing the mark either. Point made. I love you! Whatever that means!

A Sense of Humor

Paradise is composed of both words and silence. Contrary to common belief, both smiles and tears are at home in paradise. In paradise we learn that neither Truth nor Falsehood can be taken too seriously or too lightly. The Cosmos has a sense of humor. When I lack a sense of humor, I am the Alien, the one who is alienated from that union of self and world which cannot be broken. We need to laugh to see the connection. One does not see the connection and then laugh. It takes a sense of humor, which actually is a sense of balance, to meet mystery with a ritual. The humorless can't see. They would look at Uluru, the ancient ritual stone of a so-called primitive people and feel nothing. You don't have to be there or even know of that Rock. Uluru too is not a place. Uluru, too, is within.

The Dreamtime

Dreamtime. Creative time. Original time. The Moment Before the Moment. The Moment of Creation. And more. The Dawn of Time resides here. The truth be told, you are standing at the front porch of time. Here, Time stands still. The Cosmos is Time's porch. Never mind Uluru the Rock. Look within.

A Watershed Difference In Rituals

Ecclesiastical ritual in the past has been concerned with the immortality of the individual. Today a second concern may be gaining equal primacy, to care for this earth as well as for heavenly concerns. To the "primitives" of Uluru, the immortality of the tribe counts far more than individual immortality. Life matters here, on this earth. In fact, by one account of "primitive" lore, God addresses the individual soul in a cavern of Uluru after death with but one question: will you show more kindness when you return to earth? If the answer is Yes, the soul returns through lovers that night.

If No, the "hell" of those deprived of the love for life, eternal boredom is that soul's penalty. While we may busy ourselves saving our souls at the possible cost of losing or destroying the whole world, the "primitive" saves his soul by being kind to the earth. The immortality of the land is the immortality of their people. Are we not learning this lesson today? Hopefully, in time? And the primitives of Uluru live in a rather inhospitable part of our rather hospitable planet by our reckoning of values: harsh desert. What is driving us to change our comparatively rich land into desert? Or are we finally experiencing a change in values, a balance, where the ancient and modern rituals may meet and utter the same cry, "Saved!" In Time.

**What
Is
A Formal
Ritual
To
Do**

In a sense, a ritual cannot be a ritual until it is ancient. It is ancient when generations and generations of time have passed, and lessons are still being taught as they were in times passed. Not dogmatically but reflectively. Old age is the key. When our people arrive at old age, they are rarely considered contributors of knowledge or wisdom to the current time. Old age is lost upon us. It is our loss. What can be more "brand new" than a truth that one can still reflect upon, children that we are of that aboriginal dreamtime long thousands of years ago? Perhaps only old men and old women should be our priests. Just as the old men still are the priests of Uluru. There will be change. But change is one of those ancient unchanging truths. We need story-tellers of ancient stories, singers of the song-chants of wisdom, mystery, birth, death and renewal. Every aspect of the modern-day Judaeo-Christian-Muslim-Hindu-Buddhist mystique is found here at Uluru, Ayers Rock, this "primevil" place. Perhaps all the worlds' religious leaders could gain from a few hours of silent reflection at the foot of Uluru. Asking themselves what they have been about, they are bound to answer simply and in unison, "We have tried to explain the inexplainable, to ennoble the otherwise ignoble." What else is a ritual to do?

**We
May
Silently
Reflect**

We may silently reflect even if our leaders won't. We will listen to the Dreamtime story of others with an ear for recognizing common strains in the music, common struggles to resolve the enormous identity problem we are each of us stuck with by reason of being alive at all. We will listen humbly, without passing quick judgement on either our "modern" or our "primitive" selves. For we humans are many different "selves," singing not in a monotonous single tone but in a great and magnificent choral and symphonic drama. We are not black or white but colorful. We listen. We listen for the sound of our own voice. "The music of our own sphere." Imagine an old "primitive" priest sharing this mystery with you. See if you can recognize your mystery in his mystery. Just whose mystery is it? Belonging to us all, it belongs to no one. There is but one sphere. Uluru is singing our song.

The Song Of Uluru (With Guitar Lacking Didjeridoo)

Humbly I chant of the One who is holy,
*   The Knower residing in Uluru Valley,*
*   Whose sign is the Rainbow that arches the sky,*
Knower of all that will live and will die.

This is the chant of our Creator, Mother
*   Of all those Good Spirits, no two like each other*
*   Who sparkled as Lights in the Dark of Creation,*
Heroes with God in the Birth of this Nation.

Lights that remained on this Earth that they made
*   To cheer in the work of the Earth-Mother's spade;*
*   What luck it has been that our God chose to dwell*
Here in this place between Heaven and Hell!

Earth-Mother formed all the Shades in that Dawn
*   Who might become Children of all Earth would spawn;*
*   Each Child of the Dreamtime has much still to learn:*
Thus to that Mother each Shade must return!

Shades that return to the Source-Of-All-Life
*   Must learn to live better: More peace and less strife;*
*   Each shade who resists this from one life to the next*
Tosses in Boredom, eternally hexed!

Shades that are hexed are not soon Born Again,
*   They wait for the Cleansing of Ritual Men*
*   Who paint themselves proper in red and white clay; to*
Ransom such souls they must chant, they must pray.

Soothing God's wrath, if the Cleansing's done right,
*   Each Shade will return through two lovers that night:*
*   The Reason for the Chant that the Elders now sing?*
Reincarnation's the point of the thing!

Live we our lives now, serenely content
That this life we share is the way it was meant;
Secure in our faith, it's the Truth that we know,
Faithful to God is the way we will go!

Often when life seems to end at a wall,
We lean upon God and the walls always fall;
These chants full of Power and Love and the Truth
Charm even God both to listen and do!

Night comes and Sleep comes and Visions arise
To haunt us and pull us from earth toward the skies;
Awakened at dawn as we quicken our pace,
Filled are our souls with Divinity's Grace!

Pause now and leap beyond time, beyond place:
Religion and Sacrament, God leaves the trace
Each people can follow wherever they live:
Changed but in form, the same gift does God give!

After
Thought

But what do we know of our origins anyway? Nothing. Less than nothing. Scientific and Scriptural deliberations have at least one thing in common with the aboriginal chants: they are locked in mystery.

The aboriginals needed Faith to see their beliefs through the enormous vault of the centuries. Chances are that their chants will still hold meaning for someone, somewhere in the Great Outback, long after all determinations concerning our mighty origins have been lost in the not-so-grand finale of our civilizations. The reason? The aboriginals have never attempted to prove anything to anyone else but themselves.

One humble moment of Silence before that Great Mystery we try so hard to own can bring enough meaning into one's life as would render the actual first moment of creation by anyone's account to be downright dull. For we are here! Here is handle and mystery enough!

Which brings us back to the Solitary Witness, the Origin of origins, for Whom the beginning was anything but Dull, simply because, after all, the Being was there! And the handle was uneasy in the hands of the One from whom all others aborned!

III
The Meaning of Life

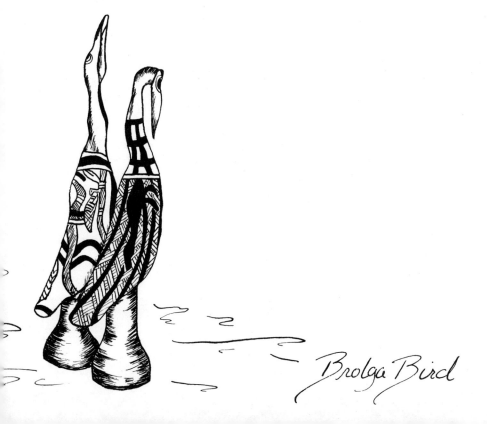

Brolga Bird

What's
The
Bloody
Meaning
Of It All

Living in a small Australian town demands of people that they make their own fun, give their lives meaning. The following ballad was written by an Aussie to give the citizens of one such town, Tennant Creek, something to sing about, something to help them get through one more week, one more day:

THE BALLAD OF TENNANT CREEK

This bloody town's a bloody cuss
No bloody train, no bloody bus,
And no-one cares for bloody us
In Tennant Bloody Creek.

No bloody clouds, no bloody rain,
No bloody curbs, no bloody drains,
The bloody Council's got no brains
In Tennant Bloody Creek.

Just bloody heat and bloody flies
The bloody sweat runs in your eyes,
And when it rains, what a surprise
In Tennant Bloody Creek.

The bloody roads are bloody bad
The bloody folks are bloody mad,
They make the brightest bloody sad
In Tennant Bloody Creek.

The bloody goods are bloody dear
A bloody buck for a bloody beer,
And is it good, no bloody fear
In Tennant Bloody Creek.

The bloody flicks are bloody old
The bloody seats are bloody cold,
You can't get in for bloody gold
In Tennant Bloody Creek.

No bloody fun, no bloody games,
No bloody sport, no bloody dames,
They won't even give their bloody names,
In Tennant Bloody Creek.

The bloody dances make you smile
The bloody band is bloody vile,
They only cramp your bloody style
In Tennant Bloody Creek.

The best place is in bloody bed
With bloody ice upon your head,
You might as well be bloody dead
In Tennant Bloody Creek.

These sentiments, lightly taken as they are, need not be limited to Tennant Creek. Nor do we have to search the byways of New York, London or Timbuctoo. These sentiments can be found in me, they can be found in you. We have asked it of ourselves many times and in many ways -- just what is the bloody meaning of it all?

Toward
An
Answer

The answer may be found somewhere in the vicinity of happiness. The problem of life's meaning is inextricably tied to life's happiness. We are all, seemingly, unwilling to admit that we are happy even when we are. The reasons for this are many. Many of us associate happiness with total joy. This can produce its own misery. It is the nature of our sadnesses that is misunderstood.

Happiness
Is The
Norm

Too often, we seem to live on the outskirts of happiness. Periodically, we touch base with some mysterious centeredness within us, and we feel glad that we were born. But there is only one "centeredness" at all and whether we are aware of it or not we are well within that strong constant's flow. Foolishly, we are ever looking for something else. What we seek is what we have. We have much to savour in what we are. When "what we still can be" arrives, it will still be what we are then. We savour what we are so rarely that when we do, we think of it as unusual. But such a savouring should be usual. Happiness is the norm, not the exception. We have ingeniously invented outside interferences and inside disturbances to this happiness as though misery were our lot and we wanted to prove it. Misery is no more our "lot" than happiness. "Is" is our lot. And at such periodic and rare moments when we think we are "in touch" we misconstrue this exceptional sensation as happiness. It is actually our "run-of-the-mill-lifeness" or beingness surfacing by our own accidental act of will or by virtue of another's act upon us. Someone lets us know by an act of generosity that he or she cares and we feel so good that we think "Aha!" "So that's happiness." Rarely do we sustain such "happiness" for long.

Happiness Is An Activity

In the eye of that mystery, in the constantly dispersing stillness, in that fullness to which consciously or not we are contributors, by an awe-filled act of synergy or integral wholiness, we intuitively marry our hearts to our intellects and achieve an awareness of yet another marriage: that of our integrities to the integrity of the universe. In such a manner is sustained "happiness" activated, cultivated, celebrated, even in the hot rushes of pain and deep furrowed sadness. We human beings must pay a price for our ability to experience consciousness. For while earthquakes do not cause felt anguish among the broken rocks, hearts do feel anguish if not break. Thus, sustained happiness is not something that is given to us. Sustained happiness is an ongoing activity requiring cultivation, demanding celebration. This is what lies essentially at the heart of a worship service, no matter the religion involved, if that religion is involved in life, as most religions are morally obliged to be involved if they live up to their truest origins. This "activity" only reflects the ongoing activity of the universe. It can therefore be said that the universe is happy.

Our Natural State

Such sustained activity appears beyond, yet is sensed within each individual's experience. We acknowledge that ours is a feeble attempt, but it is an attempt nonetheless, to match the universe in sustained becoming. By that feeble attempt, we may ennoble our frail mortality. Without marriage, there is nothing. Marriage is the thing. Not marriage as a legal document, but marriage as the ability to relate to self and world. Our sustained rejection of the integrity of the universe shrinks and demeans us. Nothing demeans the universe. Such sustained rejection is a self-imposed ridiculousness without laughter. Yet, sustained grandeur is our natural state, a condition we can share with the cosmos with complete humility.

A Word-Canvas Of Happy Days

There are particularly happy days which we remember fondly and perhaps if I share with you a few such days of mine painted in a word-canvas, you will better understand happiness as a sustained activity. In each example I will share, sustained awareness allowed me to experience growing experiences along with deep peace and inward joy.

The place: Sausalito, that lovely town on the rocks across the bay from San Francisco. On this particular day, I witness an undiminishable scene, a vision of taken-for-granted delights that seem to come out of somewhere and into nowhere. At least thirty sailboats, yachts, stand perfectly still while the sea moves under them. Then, voices, "I know what you mean, jelly bean!" Two boys and two girls, apparently more than happy to be here, eyes alert for what their hands can grab - a snail, a crab, a frog, or in that last resort, a shell or stone. I, grown up that I am, grasp for what cannot be touched, the ethereal, and I wonder why I am always waiting for something. Suddenly, one of the boys cries out, "Hey! There's a starfish!" One of the girls, "Come here, starfish! Come on!" One of the boys, "If it comes up here I'm gonna get it!" The other boy, "Can a starfish sting?" Now, an adult voice, apparently Mom, responds, "Sure can!" "Where?" "All over." "That does it! I don't want it!" "I ain't gonna pick up that thing!" I wondered, knowing that there are real dangers in the sea, just how many "stings" were adult-invented to break the dull "monotony" of peace, beauty, relationship and belonging.

Then I glanced to my left .... pillars of a long gone pier. Stung, perhaps, by a storm it did not ask for, or time. To my right, the City, pulling out from the clouds. So much like love. Love and the City. Hidden by clouds, unseen yet right before your eyes. Each morning, the mists take their blessed time undressing the city while the city dresses. Soon, the cloud lifts, startles the hills with a blue shine, replaces the shroud with bent over pieces of cloth on a thousand pieces of wood. Love, like the City, like the sea, rises but once from the slumber of my cloudy mind. If I see her, I fall in love. She sees me! And our whereabouts no longer hidden, the cloud becomes unknown!

One day in San Francisco is an existentialist's dream. At the Maritime Park bench, a young lady's life assumes its own meaning as she performs calesthenics in her yellow bikini. Half-way between her and the waves, an old man lies sleeping on a beach, dreaming perhaps of girls on a beach. A few yards further, a half dozen lithe and naked girls and boys bask in the sun despite the cold wind, taking for granted the nakedness that will someday be a source of shame. Elsewhere, shameless, at a cable stop, a pink-clothed woman sings arias from the opera *Barber of Seville*. Nearby, a young man, playfully talented, pretends shyness as he accepts the applause of those who appreciate *Fiddler on the Roof*. With his young son's help, he counts the money in his hat. Horray! Enough gratitude from his listeners to give them an encore! And I wonder - should I tell all these people that they are existentialists? I had better not! They might all disappear! Poof! Into the cloud!

Who
Might
I Be

As a young man who left home at thirteen put it: "I was, after all, faulted into a time stream without my permission. Before I knew it, I emerged, not knowing what I could do. The first outside force I knew was parental. Apparently, I was given a name and expected to live. How I would live was left up to me. A most generous twist, for while the force of my parents' will attempted to shape what was becoming of me, I found that unbecoming, and fortunately, at thirteen, in the Force's own name, I sought to discover what I could do, and thus learn who I might be."

Know
Thyself

This is the story for most of us, though for many of us the Great Risk takes place much later than age thirteen. For some, this never takes place. The wisdom of that Philosopher's exacting words shine through challengingly here: Know Thyself! But when? When do we ever really know ourselves? That's easy - one never knows until one knows that one never knows. Then, self-knowledge reveals itself for what it is - Life the Happiness Grabber!

Happiness
Prevention

Perhaps a suitable epitaph to be written over our western heads someday in a vast cultural burial ground will read, "They prevented their own happiness." Happiness prevention. I practiced Happiness Prevention when I visited the Fiji Islands. It rained on my first day in paradise! The Fijians? They couldn't have been happier. It was their first rain in three months. It wasn't just that they needed the rain. They would have been just as happy with another day of sunshine.

Out Of
Beer
Out Of
Happiness

If happiness is not the meaning of life for sentient, aware, and knowledgeable beings, what meaning will be worth it? But until my happiness cannot be washed away by an unwanted rainstorm, and until in the middle of a snowstorm, clutching my last bottle of beer, I can still be happy, then I and my happiness are at best, wishy-washy.

**Life's
Hidden
Meaning**

Several thousands of miles later, in the charged atmosphere of the Australian top-end, in Arnhem Land, I experienced a day of great happiness on a safari, even though I had to rise from bed before dawn. Pickaninny dawn that is. Which is that false dawn before sunrise when all nature is alert, after which it appears to sleep, while man and woman claim alertness. That day, the splendid creatures of that Land seemed to know I was coming. I might have stood before the whole of life's meaning without knowing it. I felt it's presence. I tried to comprehend:

**Morning
Becomes
Arnhem-Land**

*At pickaninny dawn, the mists often play
Midwife to nature's frolick, a slight, chill delay
To the heat of the big Dawn which fills Darwin's day,
When all creatures may be caught right where they lay!*

*Two dinghoes, at breakfast on a cattle side, shorn
By some sleepy driver some hours before morn,
Nibbling contentedly between thigh and horn,
Dash to the trees; leave the tragic bull torn.*

*Wallabies scatter in a light, lifting dance,
Their eyes bright with sunshine, a sight to entrance;
Shameless, exhuberant, you see them by chance,
Your pulse beat? It quickens! For sure, it's romance!*

*Then how may I speak of the songs of the birds?
Whose species, whose beauty, fall far short of words?
Bold Brolga, Ibis, Heron and Tern, such herds
Of birds that whistle hula and mock what's heard!*

*Buffaloe, not bison, roam Marrakai plains,
With power and grace that so seldom remains
In the fortunate humans who glimpse of their manes
As they wallow, by right, in safari lanes.*

*Only part of what's teeming alive is seen;
The ants have cathedrals! But what do they mean?
Mystery in abundance is sensed thick, not lean;
What is life's meaning? It's buried in the scene!*

And how do you recover what is buried? Do you dig it out? How do you dig out a meaning so closely intertwined with that which is there that to isolate its meaning is to destroy the place where the meaning is hidden? Do I really ask the

Brolga bird, "Why do you have such an elaborate courtship dance?" What would the Brolga bird say? I think I know. Because I asked. The bird ignored me until I was out of sight and wondering if indeed the Brolga does such a thing at all, after which, without the benefit of my analysis, thank you, his courtship would resume! It is like asking a man or a woman, "Why are you getting married?" Any response to that question, apart from deep or high laughter, would be to disjoint any reason well outside of its worth. Love, like happiness, is the equal meaning of life. And love is exactly spelled out in nature, in her every phase from evolution to extinction. It is only when we insist on allying ourselves on the side of what we can understand that we begin to dwindle toward the extinction of our own meaning. It is only in surrender to mystery that she reveals herself, removes her seven veils, and lets us see her as she is: A Brolga bird, doing what Brolga birds do, never mind why.

Our Destiny

Yet, we must wonder, and play with words, and pretend satisfaction with our temporary certainties until such time as the ultimate veil is lifted, and through death, we come to embrace our permanent doubts. Thus will we learn to rest our minds, not in permanent certainties, but while we live, in temporary doubts. There is our "peace on earth." There rests our "good will" toward all beingness. There is our true freedom which allows us to associate the meaning of our temporary sojourn as conscious beings with that most intimate of all rituals: care. Once we are alert to the grand web of inter-relationships which binds all beingness together, the objective, the sustaining, the all-embracing meaning of life becomes manifold. We are destined to care for all beingness.

And if at times we feel that beingness owes us some caring in return, it is then that we can remind ourselves of the good citizens of bloody Tennant Creek, and be grateful for the air we breath. The breath of life is its own reward. Having as yet nothing to compare it to until I join the other side of my given reality, I will accept life and be happy even in the most depressing moments of this side of my reality.

I wonder. In that heaven of eternal happiness, will we be asked but one question at those pearly gates? If so, that question might very well be, "And did you prevent your own happiness and the happiness of others?" I dare not imagine what punishment would fit such a crime, but hell would probably do just fine!

IV
The Front Porch Of Time

Fiji Woodcarving

Outback
Time

Flying low over the desolate landscape of the outback, I began reflecting upon time:

> Snakes of Rivers no longer wet,
> Ridges of stone no life beget;
> Dryness of brown in varying hue,
> Spotted but rarely with pools of blue.
>
> Oceans of life left behind on the Reef,
> Where are the green lands? Who was the thief?
> How fertile crescents can be filled with sand:
> Time alone knows the secret of this land.

What
Time
Is It?

The next time someone asks you, "What's the time?" and you answer, "I don't know" you are probably approaching the truth of the matter.

Time is an important matter, but one could just as easily and truthfully say, "This land alone knows the secret of time."

In other words, no one is talking. Not the Land about Time. Not Time about the Land. We are left hanging between the two, quite literally, for the Truth about these two essences so essential to our existence will never be completely known by us. Which is fair. After all, we only live here.

But we must refresh ourselves with some timely considerations. Let's do so knowing precious well that the way we pass our time surpasses any of these considerations in importance.

Time
Aside

Was Time an elaborate invention, or the by-product of one? Did Time require a brilliant act of Creation or was it just an aside, something that only came to be because something else came to be, something which did not precede Time, but came at once, not as "with" Time, but because of Time, in a grandiose simultaneity? Perhaps. Perhaps Time was the condition needed for the appearance of beingness, while that very beingness was the condition needed for the appearance of Time. And the Universe was taken by surprise, for the Universe needed such a mutual orgasm to recognize its own "isness." The Universe, Time and Beingness flow as one. Written into the lifeblood of this Beingness is Change. Thus, Beingness was the only invention. Through Change, Time and the Universe are kept alive and restless even as the perpetual calm of Assurance hovers overs and gently touches the most perilous changes wrought in time. Individual beings may die, but Beingness always wins.

Solitary Invention

Beingness was the solitary invention. With beingness and concomitant change, "is", "was" and "to be" became one with the reality of the Universe. Time is but the layers of essences manifesting themselves in all their possibilities. If there were no possibilities, there would be no time. And it is in the nature of essences to manifest themselves and to pursue possibilities. Thus, "the only true permanence is change."

Demanding Virtue

Yet, resistance to change is a demanding responsibility, a virtuous pursuit. Through periodic resistance to change, Beingness keeps a soft though rough balance among all its opposites. For Change and Permanence are not all that opposite. They are more like understanding cooperators with a lusty sense of humor. Indeed, only in sudden and major upheavals, such as earthquakes and revolutions, does it appear as though a choice must be made. The wise man or wise woman makes no choice in panic but weighs conditions before acting as a vehicle of change or as a vehicle of permanence, knowing full well that one can be either and is in oneself both. In more content and blissful times, gaps within such distinctions appear too close and an apparent time of tranquility results. Tranquility is the most effective transformer of events, since change can then take place without a ruffle, slowly, but surely. Whereas warring or traumatic times often bring about resistance to change since the concept of winning is tied to the whole matter of power and power is interested only in itself. No one ever comes into power to surrender power. While those who understand may surrender their power and become powerful indeed. "If you really want to enslave a man, free him." In such a manner, opposites serve one another in the balance to the benefit of all beingness.

Discernment Required

To many, these appear to be times of Chaos. Yet, until the meanings of Tranquility and Chaos are observed and comprehended in their essences, each in their individual "isness," in their beingness, in their relative condition, aware beings will never quite comprehend this mystery which we are so inadequate to explain, this mystery which we must attempt to discern, simply because we must discern our own meanings. We cannot discern our own meanings without understanding something of the sense of time.

**A Sense
Of Time**

Time and Timelessness are not opposites, but one essence seen as two because Change does tricks to the imaginations of aware beings. Our management of time into components of moments does little justice to the character of time. Put in terms of human awareness from which the problem of time stems, perhaps we can best relate Time's character to the human terms of "happiness" or "unhappiness" rather than to the human terms of "hours" or "lack of hours." In fact, there may be a cross-relationship here. Timelessness or a "lack of hours" is usually experienced when humans are "happy" while the full weight of "hours" or Time is felt when humans are "unhappy." When we are happily active, we say "My how time flies!" or "Time flies when you're having fun!" A sense of timelessness occurs. For example, I have experienced sheer timelessness while photographing mist-sprinkled autumn leaves on an early morning excursion into the woods. On my knees photographing close-ups, I would finally stand and to my surprise the sun would be setting. I have also experienced this same exquisite timelessness while snorkeling in the coral reefs off Maui. I experienced the darkening of the waters brought on by sunset seemingly shortly after entering the waters at mid-afternoon. A sense of time appears to be the direct result of unhappiness. When time seems to fly and we are still unhappy it is only in retrospect that it flew; actually, it "dragged." The happy are not aware of flight at all. They only observe the consequences of lapsed time, see such consequences, and "present" themselves on. Time "passes" but they do not mourn.

**Lapsed
Time**

The consequences of lapsed time are as the phases of the moon: impenetrable, unnoticeable, yet clearly visible to those who can think of a "past" and remember, think of a "future" and predict, even though the "present" gives but one phase to the naked eye. The mind makes the difference in one of two ways: by asking what happens or by asking how it happens. The asking of "why" actually goes beyond the mind, or better, carries the mind into metaphysical considerations. Such metaphysical considerations are seemingly inimical to the scientific stance. As many philosophers have observed, one can see "what" happens to the moon without regard to any explanations, as animals do. One can study and learn the phases of the moon as humans have while remaining merely polished and highly educated animals. To ask "why" can lead to heavenly assumptions, to satanic intrigue, to superstition, to fear-based religion, to magic, to consequences of lapsed time too related to power to be metaphysical in the best sense of that term. The "best" sense would respect the religious and the scientific stance without forcing humans to do the "splits" between them. Metaphysics would then be the humble acceptance of the awe of the universe while attempting to bridge the gap between ourselves and that mystery.

Memory Lapses

From such lapses of time we tend toward lapses of memory. Those who ask "why" often forget the "how" and the "what." In any case, such questions point elsewhere, toward a single, silent, yet ever pertinent question which stirs the gut and thrills the nerve. Its answer is as wordless as the question. When the answers to important questions are too certain, the memory lapse occurs. What is forgotten is the mystery which, as soon as it is explained, achieves the highest degree of doubt. We tend to accept one of two answers "just to get it over with." We either accept an answer with a possibly misunderstood scientific premise, or an answer with a metaphysical premise to which too much credibility is given. Either way, what suffers is Truth, mystery's alter-ego.

Tumbling Question

But as long as we admit that we are trying to use words not to resolve the mystery but to make us appreciate mystery's presence, well, we can playfully and lightheartedly try to ask a "pertinent" question just to see what we learn about ourselves. Such a "pertinent" question becomes a tumbling one which rolls like the sea:

> To what do we owe the ever present consumption of moments which appear to reduce our lives even as it increases our choices? Can we account for the First Time? What could possibly pass for the Last Time? Do people run out of time, or at last will time run out of people and return to that Moment before the Moment? What is this swirl which in ever dizzying doses causes life-affirming beings to die, like it or not? In the first moment of decay after the apparent death of a conscious physical being, does one's temporal mode leap into another dimension of Beingness as though all essences were in the service of consciousness, or is it only here, when all beings run out of time, that equality holds court

*as the only substantial truth? Is there no other marvel
but the marvel of this time because we are in it? Is there
then no reason to think of any other beings, past,
present, or to come, but ourselves? Do we stand on the
front porch of time as though entering or leaving? And
what is it that we enter or leave? Timelessness? And
what is eternity? Must we merely stand there on that
porch all our lives, barely knowing who or what we might
be, cowed down in the service of a Mystery we are
forever kept from knowing? Or are we that Mystery, or at
least partner to it, foolishly running away from our own
overwhelming glory as aware beings because we are
constantly looking elsewhere and never finding what we
are and have? Who keeps us from our own mystery and
why?*

Thus do we reverse the metaphysical object, until from the
deep beyond it returns to us and lays full responsibility for
our own peace and understanding right here, on this side
rather than the far side of the Grand Design.

**Sands
Of Time**

Time. Friend and thief. Lender and borrower. Tells nothing.
Leaves us in our inquisitive lurch. To flounder on dry land.
To determine or not determine as we will. At Ayers Rock, I
felt that I stood at Time's front porch. Not on it. At it. I'm
not sure where that left me. I've long since shaken the sands
of Time from my boots. I might add - with some respect.
And I've never ceased to wonder: if Beingness is served,
and if an aware being's first and most precious gift is knowledge, what have I learned?

**Lessons
Written
In Sand**

I have learned that to apreciate Time, I must first appreciate
that First Being. If Beingness was the only invention, and if
we are each of us somehow an image, a reflection of that all
encompassing Beingness which preceded all beingness,
what then is this thing we call "evolution?" After all, the
word "evolution" together with the word "genesis" conjure
up a sense of opposites rather than the seemingly necessary
simultaneity. The "evolution" people and the "genesis"
people have carried on a war on the subject of creativity for
years. What might Time say on the matter? With Time's
sense of humor, let's wonder.

**Evolution?
Genesis?**

According to the "evolution" people we are all descendants
from a lower form of life. According to the "genesis" people

all beings were created by the Supreme Being through a specific, direct and conscious order in each instance of beingness locally expressed in substantial form. The "evolution" people appear to bend toward a haphazard sense of direction out of which humans might or might not have evolved. The "genesis" people imply that the Supreme Being knew all along what He was doing. It might be advantageous to point toward a harmony between these two theories, a harmony that could enlighten us to see Time as the Laboring Room of Creation, as the Creative Tool which coalesces and disturbs beingness away from Stagnation and Unbecomingness.

Change

Change is the direct action of Time and beingness. The question remains: what being was that simultaneous brother and sister to Time? And further, what might we learn about ourselves from such a conjecture?

Conjecture

Let us dare to place ourselves in the possible frame of mind that the Origin of origins might have had in that first moment of creation. The following is pure conjecture on my part. But a rather interesting thing happened as I wrote the following words and put them in the mind of God at creation's first moment:

> **Nameless archetypal essence**
> **Protuberance from the eternal glow**
> **Extend beyond your solitude**
> **Know the aloneness of consistency**
> **As you move relentlessly toward otherness!**
> **Burst the chambers of your togetherness**
> **Become light for that rich empathy**
> **Ever seeking the brilliant, the rude —**
> **Fear not what you shall come to know**
> **As your many selves progress!**

The interesting thing that happened was a conjecture within the conjecture. No sooner had these previous stanzas come to my searching mind when I felt the inexplicable need to rephrase the verses in the following manner, giving them still another sense, with the first line followed by the last line, etc. Now, God's shout would be:

Nameless archetypal essence,
As your many selves progress,
Protuberance from the eternal glow,
Fear not what you shall come to know!

Extend beyond your solitude,
Ever seeking the brilliant, the rude —
Know the aloneness of consistency,
Become light for that rich empathy!

As you move relentlessly toward otherness,
Burst the chambers of your togetherness!

Then ....

Then, God watched and waited. In infinite patience. To see and experience forever the results of that Great Risk. For by a Direct Act of Creation, Evolution was made. That First Being which was Brother and Sister to Time was whatever became forth from whatever the Nature of that First Pro-turberance might have been.

And with it, Time, which for us conscious beings serves as an elipsis of needs in which events are chronicled as though taking place with sequence and consequence. Perhaps they were and are and ever will be. This escapes us. This is Time's Great Secret. This is our Missing Link.

**Time
Serves**

Time serves me until I sentence myself to an over ardent and sustained interest in Time. Then I serve Time. After all, the unravelling of the mysteries of life, with all its associations with meaning, happiness, purpose and redemption is tied irrevocably to the rising and the setting of the sun. I have seen many unusual sunsets in my life. A sunset can be provocative and deserving of lasting affection. I have seen such sunsets over the rooftops of Paris, the seven hills of Rome, the Matterhorn, the castle of Salzburg, the gardens of Florence, the spires of New York overlooking that apparent tranquility of the Park, the tranquility of the Redwoods and Mt. Tamalpias overlooking the spires of San Francisco; I have witnessed the sun's glow in the evening over both worlds of Disney where I often go to indulge my fantasies back to reality in a hurry, and of late, I have been wooed by sunsets on Sydney Bay, and dreamlike Tahiti, not to mention the miracle-sunsets at Ayers Rock. Yet I long for the best sunset of them all — tonight's! For I am still alive, and would count all my life's disappointments a small price to pay for one more dawn, one more sunset, one more day! Here! Wherever I am!

Fiji Islands Time

For most of us in the West the concept of time is soundly wound up within the fabric of work and responsibility to others who reward for work. The passage of days and nights alone does not seem to sufficiently inaugurate the operative condition of time. To many Judaeo-Christians, there are times to sleep, times to work and times to play, times to make love and times to make war, times to live and times to die. To the Oceanic mind, reflected in a most refined and joyous manner in so many of the Fijian natives, the "work ability" of time cannot be taken too seriously. Even as the Fijian performs a full day's task for a full day's pay, there is a playfulness in the work. While accepting White Man's Time, the Fijian also treasures his or her own sense of time all at the same time. The Fijian often surprises visitors to their islands for as he or she works, he or she exhibits not only admirable efficiency and expertise, but a highly playful, serene, sometimes heady disposition one could easily call a sense of fun.

A Sense Of Fun

I watched with a little envy the class and distinction with which the native Fijian poolside bartender at a resort served his guests. Noticing an older lady appearing somewhat "down" he called out to her, "No one should ever be sad in Fiji!" He took his now empty tray and let it sail, bumpety-bump across the Olympic pool. No one was in the water but I wondered if there would be complaints to the manager. Well, there weren't any. A few little boys and girls challenged the bartender to a short saucer-throwing contest. He accepted. It only went on for a few minutes but we were all smiling and laughing again. Including the older lady. The manager, hearing the racket, came to poolside, applauded and laughed, and left. The bartender returned to work and I wondered about Time and what it's for and I conclude that Time is for Fun, even if I must work around it.

Time And Age

One of the most obvious effects time seems to have on humans is aging. In Fiji, aging does not seem to be a result of the passing of time as the result of the passing of respon-silbilities. It is not a sense of age one sees in Fiji at all. One sees instead a sense of respect for what a person has seen and experienced, accomplished and learned. Chiefs are not respected because they have wrinkles but because they are chiefs. I observed this at the "meke" or tribal feasts and dances I attended. Age is a badge of honor worn proudly by all who have learned from life and this badge of honor is passed on at varying stages to all the younger members of the tribe. Thus, at a "meke" one senses that tribal lore has been passed on through song and ritual from hundreds of ages past right up to the present and what one reads on their faces, no matter their age, is this — smile! All life is one life everywhere! What my grandfather has my father has too and so do I and so do my children yet unborn; this is the guarantee that brings smiles to our faces: we have beat Time at its own game! We are immortal!

And indeed the beat of their songs and the beat of their music now that I think back and feel of it, was the beat of Time.

The metronome of the heart!

It's about Time!

V
The Economy of Paradise

Moorea Lagoon

Three Dollar Eggs

He was a man of about fifty-five. The Union Street bus had not yet arrived. I stood under a bus-stop cover near the wharf. It was raining. So I sat down in the protective cover of the bench. And I waited. He turned to me, his face flush with near-sobriety. Through his early morning wine, he whined. I listened, and listened, and listened. He was talking about his "truth."

"It's the truth, you know?" He offered. I couldn't resist.

"What's the truth?" He glowed in my response. He was wearing baggy khaki pants, an equally unfitting beige shirt opened at the collar, and a shabby raincoat which was more than I had considering the precipitation. He saw that I was shivering a little and offered me his coat. A little humbled, I declined. Then my lesson on the truth began.

"The truth is that this whole country is going down the garbage disposal! That's the truth. Did you know that six to eight restaurants made over $3,000,000.00 apiece last year? Did you know that? I mean right here on the wharf! And they each made three-million in their first year!"

He paused to let it all sink in. I had nothing to say. After all, I was still amazed that I had actually asked this stranger in rags the age-old question, "What is truth?" Somewhat arrogantly, I was still listening to my own voice asking the question. He went on, perhaps aware of my ineptitude.

"I tell you, if anyone ever asks you what the truth is, now you know what the truth is! The truth is found in the garbage disposals of those restaurants! The Truth is Nothing But a Bunch of Leftovers!" He chewed each word, and spat on the ground, just missing my left shoe.

"Sorry," he said.

"Nothing to be sorry about," I said.

"Those restaurants can't say that, now can they?" He waited for an answer. I smiled and said, "Nope." He seemed to like that, relaxed back and went on.

"I refuse to pay three dollars for two eggs. I don't care who laid them, two eggs will never be worth three dollars. Have you ever seen a steak worth eight dollars? I haven't! I don't care what they fed the steer! No sir! This country will soon have hundreds of thousands of people like you and people like me in the streets demanding a fairer shake. No! I don't want to be able to afford a fifteen dollar lunch! No way! It would eat a hole in my stomach! No, we're going to demand that everybody else step back a little, measure their foolish waste, and come closer to us! We don't want tc get closer to them! Nope! We want them to come just a little closer to the rest of us ... To appreciate the finer things in life, you have to go into a hole-in-the-wall .... Would you care to join me for supper tonight, young man?'' But my bus had just arrived. He read the wrinkles on my forehead, arose, shook his shoulders as if to get rid of the dust of contact with three dollars eggs, thanked me for listening and walked away.

He wasn't waiting for anything.

I was.

Honey Proper

There is the story of the aboriginal old man who lived right on top of a clear-water spring. Yet, he would always climb several hundreds of feet to a ''white man's water tank'' to fetch his water. Asked why, he would simply explain, ''White man's water better.'' Why better? Only one reason: the old man worked for a white man and part of his wages was the use of the white man's water.

Put in other words, anything that costs money has to be better.

Another story is told of the cyclone that had knocked native honey from the trees. The aboriginals wouldn't touch it. It was not ''honey proper.'' It was not the kind of honey that the black man earns wages from.

It's simple. Contact requires adaptation. Money has become an absolute essential to the aboriginal's life. From one end of Australia to the other, the economic realities of life haunted me. This ''haunt'' came from two dimensions: my own, as I slowly drew the painful conclusion that this whole world has become a tourist trap; and that of the aborigines as with ''primitives'' everywhere who must pursue their sensitive and beautiful creative abilities no longer for religious or time-honored purposes but to make a living. I was privileged to see an incredibly complicated and highly attractive aboriginal bark-painting called "Spiritual Life." In it, the artist had depicted each and everything he could remember -- ancient symbols of his tribe, Christian symbols, native animals of both the sea and the land, white people and black. To him, this was all "the spiritual life." He was ninety years old. The painting was for sale. It was priceless.

Something has been lost, I'm not sure what, both in me and in these ancient peoples. I can only grapple with the problem, after which I must let go, trusting that Time will take care of humankind, teach it "proper" lessons and that humankind will grow, not die. For now, I must save myself. The aborigine can be forgiven if that's all he wants to do. Perhaps his children and mine will know what to do. Faith in life moves me to say this. For the realities about economic-truth as shared with me by the baggy-panted gentleman on the wharf will require faith in life. Or we will despair. Faith in life is needed. The old aboriginal bark-painter had such faith. So did the tramp in San Francisco. Do I?

**To Live
In
Paradise**

The beach on the Moorea Lagoon between Cook's Bay and Opunohu Bay was literally shining in the face of the setting sun. If you have seen one polynesian sunset you have not seen them all. This particular evening was exquisite to fulness. The greens of the leaves were blinding on the palms. Though you never tire from the cavortings of the fish so close to shore, there are times when you had best leave the water and this was one of those times. I have learned to respect the oceans. So did I leave my footprints temporarily on that beach, walking into the sunset toward Opunohu Bay.

Not so innocently, I picked up one of the bamboo sticks a native family living on that beach had been using to moor their outrigger canoe. I didn't think that much of it because their canoe was out to sea and besides there were more where that stick came from. I enjoyed sticking the sharpened point into the soft sand ahead of me. I held something of this beautiful place in my hand as I walked, and that too made my walk complete.

Then I heard a shout from the sea. But it wasn't a shout at

all. It was the silence of the lagoon carrying the conversation of two fishermen to me from their outrigger as they returned to shore. As it turned out, it was the father of the family from whom I had borrowed the stick and a friend of his. I waited for them on the shore.

What followed was both enlightening and humbling.

"Hello," I ventured.

"Hello," they responded. They landed their outrigger and the net filled with what to me were strange looking sea creatures.

"Vanna," they said.

"Bob," I said, thinking they were introducing themselves.

"No, Vanna, fish for supper. Richard my name. This, Thomas. You try Vanna? Vanna good! you try!"

I couldn't say no. I did hold my breath, wondering if this was how I would end my days, eating raw flesh from freshly caught Vanna on a lovely Tahitian beach at sunset.

How could I refuse such a destiny?

Richard took the blackish colored shell of the creature, of which he and Thomas must have netted a few hundred, and breaking the shell with his bare hands, he reached within the shell for the oyster-like meat; about an inch and a half long, a half inch wide, between white and yellow, dripping with sea water. This portion of his family's supper he handed to me. What else could I do? I received it graciously, smiled my gratitude, put it into my mouth, and immediately felt a slight revulsion coming on. So I let it slip into the pouch of my left cheek. I managed to whimper, "Good!" The punishment fit the crime. Richard most generously offered a second piece. I maneuvered that bite-sized salty chew into my right cheek, turned away several yards around a cove, and let my dinner go.

Richard was no fool. On my return, he smiled, offered another dripping morsel and suggested, "Vanna in lime juice better!" I swallowed, dipped in lime juice from a lovely teak bowl. It wasn't that bad. A conversation followed, as salty in its own way as the Vanna.

"What you do in America?" He knew. I wondered if my place of origin was written all over my face. Then, I remembered. No one speaks English as Americans do.

"I teach."

"I teach too. I teach in secondary school here on Moorea. Where you teach?"

"I teach at a college." I felt warmly toward him and I wanted him to know that I liked his island. "You are lucky to be living here," I said.

"Would you like to live here?" Richard asked.

I will try to tell you what ran through my head and heart in that instant. It was despair. It was futility. It was the complete realization of my own economic reality. It was the knowledge that I could not be happy in paradise. It would require too drastic a change in my values. I knew as though my whole life were passing before me that I am too restless to live in paradise. I wanted to go home. Yet I surprised myself and heard my own voice pretending the opposite!

"Yes, Richard, I would like to live here." There is one thing more difficult to swallow than raw, salty Vanna. Humble pie!

Richard looked at me with deep understanding of my plight. Compassion shown brilliantly in his eyes. He didn't have to say anything. But he did. And I listened. To my teacher.

"This is my supermarket." He pointed to the sea. "Everyday I go find my supper out there. I not make much money. I not polished traveler like you. I simple man with simple wants. I satisfied be here. But you? You satisfied be here? How?"

"It is so peaceful here," I said. (Another helping of humble pie, please!)

"It is not peaceful where you come from? You come here for peace? Can you stand peace? Can you stand to be content with what you have? If you can, you not be here now! No matter where you go, you not content. Unless you first content at home. Maybe I be too mean. Sorry. You look like good person. But I frustrated too. I share my paradise with you. But I frustrated too. I tempted to have what you have. Now my peace bothered. Time before you come we have human sacrifice. Taboo now. New human sacrifice come! On altar of business!"

"I understand." I could only look at him in silence.

"Have some more supper!" By now, Richard and Thomas had shelled at least seventy Vanna. His wife and children joined us at the shore. We would all eat from the common bowl. I didn't hesitate. I took the smallest piece I could see, all smothered in lime juice, and swallowed it whole without chewing. "Sit," he offered. "Eat More." I couldn't. But I wondered that evening about the symbol that salt represents to so many people -- wisdom -- and I wondered if I had learned something and what.

**Lessons
From
East Timor**

The airport at Sydney, Australia. To my left, waiting for his plane, a very well dressed retiree in his seventies. John was his name. He was alone. A widower. Returning to Australia and to his home to renew his passport, he missed the enchanted land of his retirement, East Timor in the great islands of Indonesia, north of Darwin somewhere.

I asked him about his life in retirement: was it good for him? What has he learned?

"Young man," he said, "do you really want to know what I have learned?" I nodded and smiled because he was smiling too. He went on.

"The people in East Timor are so kind, so warm, so friendly. To me, East Timor is paradise. Well, at least the place where I live. I needed a climate with a constant temperature of seventy degrees, and in the valley near the foothills of majestic mountains in East Timor I have found perfect weather, perfect solitude, and perfect friends, all at once. The standard of living isn't high at all. I can live on my retirement checks there. But not here in the country where I earned my retirement."

"The people, my friendly neighbors and I, live very simply.

Without the need for air conditioning. Without television. Without the comforts of technology. We are still quite comfortable. We eat well. I never go to bed hungry. Yet by your standards, we are poor. My friend, by anyone's human standards we are rich and you are poor because we are satisfied and you are not."

There was a pause. I dared not fill that pause, nor did I know what to fill it with. He continued.

"After nearly seven years in East Timor, I can safely say to you that there are no underdeveloped versus developed countries. Oh no! Rather, with their culture, their happiness, their peace, their lifestyle, their simple lifestyle, such peoples as live in East Timor are *developed!* They are *developed!* Australia? America? They are *over-developed!* And one day, they must pay the price!"

"One more thing. You think you have corruption in your society? Watergate? Well, we have corruption in our society too. We have poor people by any standard who, like any other people, yours or ours, would like to improve their lot in life by ever so little. To buy a pig or two. A dog. A batik. To buy a mantle, a trinket, a wife. To afford a luxurious spread once in a while. And so our people, many of them, have illegal businesses on the side, selling this, selling that. Batiks. Statues. What not. The government not only overlooks this, but expects this. Your government aspires to be the pinnacle of virtue to all the world, and you bring perfectly human foibles, bothersome as they may be, into your law courts ... yet bribery never leaves your land. We have a sense of humor in this imperfect world. You don't. And do you know where this "perfection" of yours will lead you? To blow up the planet. Because it's not good enough. Well, it's good enough for me."

The call went out for our departure for separate destinations, the Great Barrier Reef, and John's Shangrila. As I boarded my plane a pleasant chill went up my spine. I suddenly remembered the words of Lao Tzu, who said: "Those who expect good government without misrule do not understand the universe." I may have just concluded a conversation with a man who understood the universe. I was haunted by the Shade of Lao Tzu!

East of Fear

Later, on my way to Cairns and The Reef, I wondered about the linguistic coincidences of life. The word "timor" in latin means "fear." Apparently, my friend from Sydney lived East of Fear.

Fear and Shadow In Paradise

It is fear and shadow for most of us. Fear and shadow, even in paradise.

Ayers Rock has a sun side and a shade side. On the shade side there is a cave of the 'Big Woman' and within that cave a 'Stone of Conception' which the tribal woman rubs if she should desire a child. On the other side, the sun side, there is a place from whence the Great Spirit sends forth spirit children to be reborn. Going forth from the sun-side of the Rock, they seek out mothers who will bear them as mortals.

The idea is as common as all humanity and is found in all religions. Children are born to women through desire. And not so hard to understand at all, the spirit of such a child is sent forth to find itself a mother from the sun side or happiness side of the mountain. But the child is born from the mother on the other side, on the side of fear and shadow.

Yet if we are in love with life, we do not spend our lives totally in the shadows. The mystery of life does not choose among such opposites as sun and shadow. Such a distinction is more poetic than real. For the sun is intimately associated with shadows. Light and darkness are not at odds. One can begin to see a glimpse of Hope which always resides somewhere between sun and shadows. I too must look east of fear.

No Worries

I am not an economist. But I am a realist. Like it or not, we are all subject to certain conditions which make our lives economics-oriented. Without some kind of economics, life is unbearable. The barter system is as old as life. Give and take may be the two ingredients of creation. Creation stumbles in the absence of either. But east of fear I see something powerful and good, yet something that frightens me for all its philosophic and economic implications.

East of fear, I see a land of no worries.

No worries.

The Americanization of paradise may be inevitable. In the parlance of the Aussie there are "no worries" about it. It's what's happening, just as anything else has "happened" in the past. Of course, we can ask ourselves, must the future just "happen?" Will any amount of tranquil refusal to worry bring any long-term good to ourselves and our progeny? I don't really know. Where did the phrase "no worries" come from? One can sense a "no worries" atmosphere among the aborigines of Ayers Rock. But they have no credit cards with accompanying temptations which lead to the inevitable debts. But I like the idea. No worries. B.C., Before Credit, what could those words mean? No worries. These words might contain a profound spiritual lesson. It may be the mind of a man or woman who really has faith. Faith in God by any name. Faith in the human race by every name. It is the mind at rest, convinced that there is no losing. Nor winning. Just being. And that this being alive is its own reason and needs no other. Faith in life.

Yet the very Americanization of paradise is nothing less than this: an introduction to the subtle art of worrying. Experience can point to our economic way as at fault. Our economic way lives on worry. Our economic way thrives on worry. It would appear that our economic way invented worry to serve its own interests, and it did so in the best example of the ethic of the ideal: Relax, You Have Master Charge. Relax? The ideal, of course, is to be independent in money matters. But are we? Were the "primitives" once the way we imagine we want to be? Independent in money matters? Why can't the richest nation on earth burn its credit cards? Because we are a people in debt. Without debt, we would be without our inventions. We are owned by our inventions. Worry follows. It's as simple and as complicated as that. Perhaps the people who believe as the Aussies seem to believe in a land of no worries have something to teach us. Perhaps we have been all too successful as teachers. Perhaps we should take turns being students again and learn from those whom we have come to teach. It may be too late. In Darwin, I saw a poster of Uncle Sam with this caption: YOU NEED UNCLE SAM!

Lessons Learned

Bill Harney, that intrepid Australian yarn teller, knows the aboriginals quite possibly better than anyone.

In one account, Bill tells of rag-covered aboriginal children, their intelligent, finely cut faces looking out from mops of sun-bleached blond hair. They are not afraid nor do they beg. If they are given suckers, they enjoy them immensely but they give the gentle air of those who could taste of another life yet still be happy with their own. It is as though they refuse to be pampered by abundance. They are a people who are at ease with themselves.

There was an explorer named Lasseter who searched the outback for gold. He failed, becoming his own symbol of the eternal quest for the illusive. By some strange modern day alchemy, we too seem to be constantly looking for anything that can translate into green gold.

But there is a richness beyond the touch of Midas.

You and I have felt such richness in moments of natural harmony. The aboriginals are quite familiar with such wealth. You can't eat gold. But spirits can feed your soul if you let them speak to you from their abode in the Rock. Lasseter perished looking for gold. Yet he would have lived, and lived quite happily at that if instead he were searching for a place filled with life.

This was a hard land and still is. The aboriginals have thrived on this land for thousands of years. Tasting the red dust as the wind seems to blow the entire desert in your face, you wonder, how did the aboriginals do it? They were not fools. They understood their land. They loved their land. And their land returned that understanding, that love and that respect, teaching the aboriginals all about itself, until, lessons learned, a happy place was theirs, a place where they could live and die with no worries. We should have so fortunate an arrangement with our bounty-filled land! To exchange roles with the earth! To let the earth shout its lessons into our ears!

VI
Shake The Truth From Your Shoes

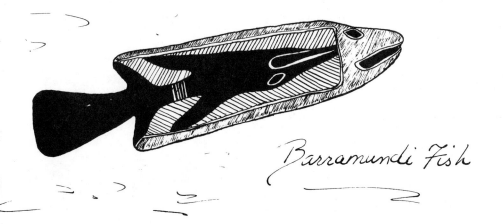

Barramundi Fish

Dust
And
Truth

Walking around the base of Ayers Rock, the hot desert sun might have had some effect on the flight of my imagination. This was a sacred walk. I knew that many an aboriginal truth was buried somewhere in the caves, crevices, shadows and protuberances. The natives still pass these truths onto their children. As I kicked the dust of the desert sands into the air ahead of me, I wondered what truths I was shaking from my hiking boots.

Then, I imagined:

The
Song
Of
Miman

I am Miman,
Who wonders, but does not wander;
Others traverse the seas
Seeking me;
I gather the seas to myself
And know the others
are me.

I am Meandor,
Time Embracer;
Though I am dearly sought
Everywhere
I cannot be found here nor there
Nor anywhere;
The Truth that I speak is a
Reflection of me:
Unfounded.

Truth, married to Time:
No wonder
Neither can be grasped
For Truth, like Time,
Is constantly sought in
Substance
While both are laughing in the shadows!
Seek not the Truth
Where Laughter is not heard!
When the dust settles,
Truth is there,
Bouncing off the rays of the Sun,
From shade to shade Truth bounces,
From dim lavender to bright orange red.

Dim Death
Dances in each shade,
And I am that shade:
Truth shines in me
Uncomfortable in the sun:
Truth warms up to me at night
When the whole earth is in shadow;
In deepest slumber I finally embrace the Truth
Unknowing.

Truth
Moves in circles
We are not accustomed to:
In the pits
Is the Truth often found;
Unless you are in the pits,
For then the Truth moves on.

I am Imbiber, Dirt Eater,
Time settles in me
Like sediment in a mountain stream;
Therefore
Hear me.
Hear my silly sounds,
For old lies bear repeating

Until the last grain of Truth
Drains out of them
And finally,
Light as air,
Time wafts them forever
Into the infinite forms of the
Unchanging,
There to receive the staid worship
Of those who cannot stand to know.
You who say you can stand to know,
Prepare your brains and hearts!
For they too are sand only
And as sand
They are fit instruments
Of what can be known:
Truth thou art,
And into Truth
Thou shalt return!

**Back
To
Earth**

The voices from my imagination receded but they made me wonder as I returned to myself again: never mind the ''voices.'' What about truth? It occured to me that perhaps the activity of seeking out the ''truth'' is too readily surrendered to others and too readily taken on by those who would master their sisters and brothers. This can be seen as both an understandable and a deplorable reality. Given enough solitariness, especially in times of upheaval, a person can conjure up from his or her own juices deep persuasions, or pursue exhausting intellectual paths on behalf of ''truth.'' Then, if they so wish, they may seek out and gain a following among those who are either too emotionally or intellectually ill-suited, lazy, or bright but easy; men and women who are willing to grab whatever responds to the moment, gives them meaning and distinction. Security disguised as Truth. Instead of life-long seekers, they become the baited. The debateable overwhelms them. Ambiguity is too much for them. But what do they know? And what have they surrendered?

**Truth
Beyond
Words**

For ''truth'' is not merely the manipulation of words. Truth is beyond words. The humble know this. But so often the manipulation of minds is joined to the manipulation of words when the right to think is limited to those in power.

**Truth
Beyond
Power**

The emergence of a majority of highly educated human beings in a society will lead to a more authentic sharing of freedom and power. When a majority of a populace becomes truly ''educated'' and ''literate'' the triangle of power's hierarchy will level off through a greater sharing of responsibility. The significance of this is most practical. There will always be those who spend their lives in study and they will always carry a responsibility to the workaday, yet educated majority. But the likelihood of being completely and successfully ruled by the faction in power will diminish greatly until the relationship between those in power and the educated majority will become more and more a cooperative relationship in self-knowledge than a battle to control others.

**Truth
Is
Sensuous**

Indeed, the seeking of truth is a sensuous pleasure not to be denied or limited to anyone. There is something delightful, even orgasmic, in the process of thinking and truth-seeking. There is a certain dimension of sweetness, a ''super'' but ''natural'' high, call it a super natural high, found in actually feeling one's thoughts grow and enlarge until they are born.

It is to be carried away by special surprises that seem to come from nowhere. To take such a trip is pure ecstasy. To share such a trip with another, without the object of winning or being right, but simply to see what both might learn: such is the stuff of peace on earth. Those who deny this, tend toward battles of another kind, where winning is essential, and being right is all there is.

Truth Is A Surrender

The pursuit of truth and knowledge are pleasures very much like the pleasures of body surfing. There is a surrender which carries you away with a loft and a drop, a smoothness and a roughness which eventually returns you to the sandy security of shore. Yet remaining unsure, though secure, you refuse to be satisfied by your first return and dip your way back to the splashes of broken answers, to the questions that are always left hanging in the sea. Questions are never resolved in the abstract while in the open sea; such abstract resolutions are possible only on dry land, where the pounding of the waves cannot remind you of your innate frailty and irresolve. Either way, the choice is clear: to experience the illusion of being in charge which the shore gives you, or to tangle with the illusion of being out of control which the ocean gives you. Where, Oh where is the notion of Truth? In the ocean? On the shore? Or is there more?

Truth Is Shy

I fear and celebrate the "more." Truth, that abysmal commodity that compares only to Love in its conch-like attraction, carries a sting along with its beauty. I fear and I celebrate that the Truth resides patiently enough, miraculously growing a magnificent and stunning shell around its tediousness, or stoking up the long, long dormant fires of its own Haleakalea, but most certainly does the Truth reside so patiently in the golden bosoms and bottoms of both genders clad in minimums barely covering the Truth. And when naked, the Truth runs for cover, not from shame, but by its very nature.

If Truth be so shy, what of Knowledge?

The Truth Is A Gnat

Knowledge is very much like the desert dust that settles in a traveler's throat like a gnat. Perhaps the Truth is a gnat, for it always seems so much smaller than we ever hoped it would be. Yet, when comprehended for what it is, the truth about ourselves, the truth about life, the truth about the cosmos, we would cease our worries about the nature of truth and confront Truth with the smallness of ourselves. For I am the gnat in Truth's throat, ever demanding more of less and less of more, never at home, at home.

Truth Is Our Home

For Truth is our home. Knowledge and truth are inseparable, and we are right at home with knowledge and truth. Why then are we never at home, at home? Why our ceaseless wanderlust that allows us to go so far away from home that we hardly ever appreciate where we are and so often ask ourselves where we would rather be? Paradise is what we claim to seek. Yet paradise is ours to claim if we could only be at home, at home.

Truth Is A Communicator

Perhaps we are restless with knowledge because what we come to learn as we grow older is so often in difficult contradiction with what we have been taught is so. Thus, the truth hurts because we are so unfamiliar with it. Yet, it is the very ground on which we stand.

There is yet another saying that familiarity breeds contempt. Consider the humbler here. If the truth is not familiar ground, yet it is the truth, just what are we unfamiliar with? What hurts us then is not the Truth, but the often terrifying fact that what we expected to be true does not agree with what we actually come to know when the truth communicates itself to us. In short, the truth does not agree with us. What it communicates does not go down well. Does this indigestion tell us something about truth or about ourselves?

Truth Is Subtle

Truth is a subtle communicator. It is obvious, then, why so few of us are receptive to the truth — we like to be hit over the head with it. We are poor communicators, poor listeners. To protect what we want to believe, we must set up defiance against the knowable. Our fear that what we could come to know will defy what we would rather believe has brought us to this. Will we ever realize the beauty of what we fear? Will we ever know the heartbeat of the cosmos if we are afraid of what we might learn? Must the fear of contradiction wipe out our lifeline to the greatest gift, the noblest imperative we are capable of, which is To Know?

Truth Is Priceless

Another reason so few of us are receptive to truth is that we don't trust what we can't buy. Enter, Hucksters of Truth. False mystics who pretend to have burst barriers of knowledge are eager to abuse the "baitable" with their misused gifts of charisma. Such mysticism is the enemy of both truth and knowledge, is not mysticism at all, and ends up being but a sickening salve which deadens an individual's capacity to know the truth. The truth is not for sale. It is like a dead cat's head: priceless.

Levels Of Learning

The human experience of learning is too often sensed at levels hardly verbalized and hardly appreciated. The senses are not limited to five but include an infinity of sensations so tied to one another that we are overcome by it all and we isolate those sensations until we can relate to them logically. But as soon as we begin to relate to them logically a deterioration begins whereby an overarching, all embracing cosmic moment dwindles in its texture to but one or two levels of receptivity, of communication, usually at the point of first contact or the surface of the experience.

Live In Character

This deprivation is utterly illogical. Why live any given moment of ordinariness without charm, without soul, without grace, without character? Especially "character." What might "character" be but the habitual state of receptivity to the total quantum of life experiences. In sum, it is the willingness to receive the truth, even if it is not what we wanted to know. It is self-neglect to be receptive to less in a moment of life then is there being given, freely, by the Force of that moment. We badger ourselves into assessing that we can only bear so much reality.

We are a people too easily overwhelmed by what is well within our grasp -- the simple understanding of our lives in the sumptuous setting of the universe. To be receptive to anything less is to live on the hide of a flea.

Truth Is Natural

Logic, a fine tool for seeking knowledge and truth, like all human tools, can easily degenerate as it often has into a tool for perpetuating the power trip, which "trip" requires that the masses must spend their lives on the hides of fleas. Logic, in the finest cosmic sense, is the experience of the ultimate syllogism, which contains no words, yet is succulently filled with the nerve-ends of profound truths; truths which are within us all because truth, as with happiness, is a natural state of life.

Page 66

Knowledge Is A Love Trip	Knowledge is not the top of a pyramid, which is to say, tied to the power trip. Knowledge is a love trip. The whole of creation is composed of Knowledge. The pyramid is but a sometimes necessary man-made device to be used for perpetuating the hierarchic structure of power as a formidable tool of the knowledgeable. But all aware beings are capable of knowledge. For this reason, the primary task of a teacher is not to pass on knowledge so much as to increase the intensity of his or her students' awareness of their own knowledgeability.
Human Community: Learning Community	The human community can no longer endure a paucity of knowledgeable people. Brilliance is not the question. In fact, brilliance can be a hindrance to knowledgeability. Buckminster Fuller is a notable exception. Fuller has said in many places and in many ways in his works that the human community needs more and more individuals who actively seek to know more and more, in many areas of learning, not as a profession, nor as a power tool over others, but as a natural inclination in life. The Trappist Monk, Thomas Merton, was an exemplar of this great passion for knowledge. Even though he was, as a monk, in no position to "use" his knowledge, it was enough that his own appreciation for the "world" he had "left" and for the earth he loved grew in zen leaps and zen bounds.
A Demanding Inclination To Learn	Nor is this "inclination" a "lazy" inclination. It is a demanding one .... demanding the reading of more than one book, exposure to more than one point of view, interest in pursuing more than one subject, and the stubborn refusal to surrender to final conclusions that render further investigation impossible. For some, their reading will be joined to first hand study of their sources, whether those sources be found in reading original works, travel, or actual scientific investigation, although the latter will rarely be the interest of non-academics.
Disinterested Interest In Truth	Perhaps we may learn from one academician the lesson of humbly active learning.

A certain professor spent many years writing a book called, "Issues in the Economics of Advertising." He concluded his 371 page book in this manner: "All this implies that that the economic study of advertising is not deserving of great attention except for special problems." Then he added in a wry parenthesis, "As the reader may realize, this is not a congenial point at which to arrive after spending several years working on the subject."

How rare, how lovely, and how utterly genuine! Most of us, dedicated for years to such a project, would tend to find more in it than was there, would puff up our conclusions and pretend that the work had some great positive value. Few would confess candidly that Truth had led them down a blind alley. Yet it is this disinterested interest in Truth that can give science its "religious" quality, and that can give religion a "scientific" quality.

Paramount Question

Which leads us to a paramount question: is knowledge ever certain and is truth relative? These are but one question. Another way to state it would be to ask: is there such a thing as objective Truth, that is, truth which stands all by itself as truth regardless of how many people believe it is so, or if none so believe?

To Surrender Our Right To Be Right

Truth will most often come to us as a reconciliation rather than as one of a pair of opposites. For example, as long as we fight over who is right, the creationists (God created the earth in seven days) or the evolutionists (life on earth came to be by natural rather than divine processes) or whether we should listen to St. Paul's advice to get to work and quit thinking about the end of the world as imminent or spend the rest of our lives pretending to understand Revelations; as long as we are stuck on such choices between apparent though not necessarily opposite opposites, we may individually win exasperating arguments, but the Truth is ignored.

For the problem about the truth is not about the truth at all but about ourselves. Consciously or unconsciously, Death is an ever present reality in our lives. One way we humans can pretend to defeat death would be to bear witness to eternal truth as if we know it, when actually, if the Truth be told, we don't.

But Truth will win. The Truth has nothing to do with us as long as we must win. But as soon as we surrender our right to be right, we are right and the Truth has everything to do with us. Once we surrender to the absolute indifference of the universe, God may finally be free to peek through those clouds of unknowing and self-doubt and allow us a glimpse of our transparent universe, where the Truth stands out for all to see: not quite as we expected, but enough to fill both the hearts of those who were so sure they knew and those who thought there was nothing to know.

VII
Death And Beauty

Moorea Seashells

The Desire To Live

The desire to live is something fierce. In the desert dry-lands of the Australian outback, life pushes itself out of the sand and stone to shout at the sun. When the sun pushes life back into the sand, just you wait and see! After a mere smidgen of a shower a tiny geranium will pop out of nowhere. In a week, it's in full leaf. Then it just stands there for lack of moisture and does nothing. As if sensing that further rain will not be coming, it does not give up on life. Out from the frail plant a tiny flower comes.

Life Goes On

Life goes on. Each plant, the servant to another life. Some desert plants have outgrown despair. They have learned, adapted, flourished, and smiled radiantly into the face of death. Death is not a part of a plant's neurosis.

The Grand Sequence

Death. Beauty. Knowledge. Change. Newness. Death. Beauty. Knowledge. Change. Newness. Is there anything else of which Wisdom is composed? We can add Compassion. Understanding follows. There are no God-forsaken places. Only God-foreseen. Every place and every situation is an opportunity-enriched place or situation, no matter how desperate it may seem to be. To the aboriginals, the desert is paradise. We, their white-skinned relatives, seem to always be looking for a better place. We are not beyond help! Like the plants, we too can learn from life. Death. Beauty. Knowledge. Change. Newness. Compassion. Understanding. The sequence that makes sense of suffering and hardship, even as it diminishes despair. We are in our glory!

The Searing Truth

Buried in Creation's heart is a searing truth: that Death and Beauty are eternally joined in a conspiracy against boredom and on behalf of Life. Beauty is what Death is all about. And this hurts. Beauty is what we can't seem to get enough of. The craving for money, fame, power and sex may very well be but one way of substituting for what we really want: Beauty. Indeed, we often pay such an enormous price for just a portion of Beauty. Yet Beauty is beyond price. Death does not give us that choked-up feeling. Beauty gives it to us. The sight of a fawn leaping through the woods allows us to level with Death and Beauty in such a way as to leap ourselves beyond fear to the full recognition that we are alive, that we are here at all. It's a miracle! The miracle of being here at all. It is what we see and know and recognize as beautiful that chokes us up inside. We are so happy that we just can't stand it. We can't stand what we can't have for keeps, in the way in which we know it. And that is the searing truth.

What
We
Can't
Have

What we can't have is what we can't be: perfect participants in Beauty's sojourn in the passage of our lives. We want a beauty that never passes and ever exceeds itself with each time of our lives. We don't want much, do we? We personalize Beauty. We deify Beauty. We dogmatize Beauty. It is pure dogma to insist that Beauty is in the eye of the beholder. Beauty is not always that carefully sliced into individual prejudices. We can all marvel at seeing the same thing. We can share awe and wonder and surprise together. And we do. Only the dullest would feel nothing standing before a herd of elk grazing in the early morning mists. We can see the beautiful together, even where we had not seen Beauty before. In Death. Or ashes on a carpet. Or a man or woman who does not quite measure up to our expectations. Too often, if our fellow humans do not measure up, God does. When God is everything we expected God to be, be assured that we have diminished God, that we have surely made God too small. Once we have put away all of our expectations, expecting nothing, we will then not be disappointed. Perhaps then we can see and appreciate Life just the way it is. Perhaps then we can see the Beautiful everywhere. Perhaps in return Life will give us what we never dared to expect: Beauty that never passes, though changed by the passage of time; changed, yet ever the same. Dependable. Liberating. Even in times of blind anguish, Beauty is there. When you think Beauty and Life have left you in a lurch, check again! It is your lurch. It has your trademark. When in my arrogance I imagine that my soul is in me, I stand to lose, soul and all. But I am in my soul! I can't lose!

The Need
To See Life
As It Is

Thus the need to see Life as it is. Not necessarily in exactly the same way, but to see Life at all, the same Life, and for what it is: Beauty in all of its manifestations. Seen in this way, Death is but the servant of Beauty.

Beyond
Opposites
To Wisdom

In the end, and from the beginning, as with all opposites, Beauty and Ugliness are no more at war than Life is at war with Death. But because we may have taken the veridical nature of Beauty for granted, misunderstanding was inevitable. As the only intellectually aware beings we know of, we human beings are both the hope and despair of Life.

We can destroy Beauty, and with it, Life. Is it that we so often destroy Life because we do not see the beauty? Can one see the beautiful and destroy its expression in life? Death does not destroy. Death is partner to this Life we see together. To destroy is an intentional act. Humans are the only intentional beings we know of. Perhaps as we move beyond opposites, seeing that all opposites are foolish distinctions anyway, we will begin to appreciate Beauty's relationship with Life and Death. We will see the beautiful in what once passed for the ugly. The only Ugliness that will be left will be that which destroys, willfully, and with set purpose; and we will move beyond such mad intentionality, recover the beauty of our intelligence, the delight of sheer being, and the hilarity of wisdom.

Earthquakes Are Not Caused By Sin

The passage of nature is not one filled with privileges for the few. To nature, no one is special. Or, if you wish, everyone is just as special as anyone. In a manifest way that can hurt the enormous Ego of an individual so burdened, nature's way is that of true equality. If an earthquake destroys a church during a Sunday service, rocks don't miss priests or saints. If all are killed, there are no survivors. No "miracles" to demonstrate the "victory" of righteousness. We all go down together, the "good" with the "bad!" And Life is served! It is part of the Commotion of Life, and nothing stops that Commotion. It is God's will, stamped forever upon everything that is. It may very well be the only truly obvious manifestation of God's will. And it would take an enormous Ego to circumvent that will and create more meanings than are already there within the Original Plan. We humans are sadly capable of such Self-centeredness. There is nothing God can do about a collapsing church building because God is not saddled with an enormous Ego. We are. God knows that eventually all things will obey the second law of thermodynamics, the supreme law of nature that never lets us forget that all things are passing. God knew that through such an eternal law of change, even people could get the message and through suffering and the symbolic deaths that suffering brings; move from the ego-centeredness that blames everything on sin to the humility that sees that we are all in this together.

Present At The Creation

Those who would like to blame sin for everything should visit the Grand Canyon and let their minds drift back to the Creation. If you had been present at the Creation of the Grand Canyon, you would very likely have screamed to High Heaven to get you out of there! Such moments of creativity are beautiful only from a distance in time, after the dust has settled, and admiration takes over as the sores of that terror-filled commotion become Beauty Marks for all to appreciate. So must we keep faith with the commotions of our lives and allow the sores and hurts of our hearts to become Beauty Marks in the course of Time. As with earthquakes, there is no avoiding the quivers of the soul as we grope and grow, become and unbecome. The happiest people on earth have accepted this. It becomes them! The rest of us are a miserable lot as we wait for Life to go our way. It has. Where were we?

The Grand Miracle Of Being

Individual life is the temporary celebration of the Grandiose Miracle of Being at all. All aware individuals can join in that celebration. All aware beings, each in their own way, can appreciate this miracle. They also appreciate the price that each must pay to celebrate that miracle: death. How a being dies is irrelevant. That beings die is of prime importance. The Grandiose Miracle of Being is not in the service of individual lives. Individual lives are in the service of the Grandiose Miracle of Being. It is precisely this reality, once accepted, which brings dignity and mystery to an individual being's life. And Faith makes the leap to the Hope that through Love that Being will return the favor, somehow, beyond this life on earth. What is of interest to aware beings is that all so-called inspired scriptures call for aware beings to love one another, and in that love here on earth, that Being is satisfied. So can we be satisfied.

Look About You

There's nothing cheap about you. You can't be spread out too thinly, squandered too thickly, or debased to the meaningless prattle of those who would have you eat, drink, and be merry. It works the other way around. Tomorrow, you will die. You may eat, drink, and be merry if you wish, but look about you at what else there is! Look about you at those other miracles of creation who do not run around as though Gluttony, Debauchery and Despair were the stuff of Life. Look around. Most other beings are not plotting wars, building tall monuments to themselves, or watching themselves make sexual hay while the cinematic sun shines. They don't have to. They have accepted their deaths. And while comparing other earth-beings to man has its drawbacks, think upon it for a minute and wonder about Man and

Woman and You.

**We Are
Naked**

Sure, unlike the rest of creation, we wear clothes. Thus do
we tempt nature and thus do we make room for pornography
as though nakedness were our natural state and we just
couldn't wait to get back to it. Well, nakedness is our natural
state. There is no need to return to our natural state completely and rid ourselves of clothes, but we can return to
that natural state in spirit, and with Death's inspiration at
our side, accept our natural nakedness with greater joy and
lesser shame. This, and this alone, can render pornography
unnecessary. We are pornographers because in our minds we
are clothed. If we were naked in our minds and could live
with it, we would come closer to our natural state, and the
so-called sexual revolution would ''climax'' in a healthy state
of cooperation between mind and body that no extreme
could pull asunder.

**Balance Is
Our Natural
State**

Sure, unlike the rest of creation, we are never satisfied in
our consumption of food, alcohol, and smoke, and things. We
even make people into things so that we can consume them
in a war as cannon fodder. Thus do we tempt nature to make
room for excess as though balance were our natural state.
Well, balance is our natural state. It is worth dying, then,
to have lived, to have loved, to have looked upon Beauty,
to have wondered about the relationship of my heartbeat
to that of the Universe! The pulse of God and your pulse:
those are enough to make you wonder, as you wander, humbly
and proudly, on the wonderful, rough edges of Life. The
soft Center awaits a reunion with you. When you return to
God, you won't be surprised to hear a thunder of applause.
And can you think of a better place for that applause to
begin than Here! Look around you! It's a miracle! Applause!

VIII
The Dreamtime of God: A Parable

God had a mind to create the universe. And God created it. God had a mind to create the earth and to fill the earth with all varieties of living things. And God created it. God had a mind to bring forth creatures who were intelligent, though not necessarily smart; feeling, and quite often unfeeling; co-creators, though certainly capable of destruction. And God created them.

All creation grew, shrank, developed, withdrew, progressed, punted, changed, and alternately surprised God with delight or surprised God with deep disappointment. God is not beyond surprise. All creation grew, shrank, developed, withdrew, progressed, punted, changed, sometimes for good, sometimes not for good, and most of the time it was hard to know the good from the not good. God determined that this was the nature of nature, since all opposites are but the alternate complementary sides of the same energy force, truly in harmony, but subsequently analyzed to death by earth intelligence. And so the war between good and evil was an unnecessary war. The energies could have been used to bring about the understanding of paradox to better understand nature, to better understand the source of nature, to get into the mind of God.

And so all creation grew, shrank, developed, withdrew, progressed, punted, changed in the mind of God. And all creation did not know it. All creation is a circle within a circle. Creator and Creation can best be described in design as a parallel spheroid, a circle within a circle. Except that God is the greater circle within which all else is.

All creation is on God's mind, depends on God's mind, will last as long as God has a mind to let it last.

Or is it the other way around?

For God is very much on our minds. We think of God when we don't even know we are thinking of God. Believers don't have an edge on anyone. All experience divine overlap on the human consciousness. In fact, there are times when one is aware of a unity of consciousness hardly different from that "other" which we cannot know from experience, yet known just as surely though from experience, although felt to be outside of experience. Cosmic consciousness is none other than infinity caught in a time warp, in which the greater circle is very truly grasped as though contained within the lesser circle, as though God's mind and our mind are of one mind, inseparable equally of consequence, mutually dependent, at once eternal and finite, forever being born for the first time, constantly dying for the last time.

And so perhaps it can be seen that God is on creation's mind, depends on creation's mind, that God will last as long as creation has a mind to let God last.

The idea that God should ever rest is thus quite frightening, as frightening as eternal rest on creation's part. Total forgetting is difficult to conceive. We say to others "forget me not" as though we know what power is in remembering, what power is in forgetting. Death means more as a forgetting than as any other possible concept. Death as forgetting. And somehow we know life as a remembering, a recognition, an ability to connect pieces, to be able to depend on relating parts to whole, people to people, yes, Creator to creation.

Life is a kind of reliability, a dependability, a trust-worthiness of people, places, and events. To go home is to go to a place you can count on. To find your lover there is far more nourishing than not to find your lover there, his or her dependability is akin to life. We can count on the sun to rise. We want to count on our friends. If we can't count on the sun, death is near. If we can't count on our friends, we feel forgotten, we feel far from life.

Should God take creation for granted, creation dies. Should creation take God for granted, God dies, of course, this "death" of God is not a literal death, but is relative to ourselves. It is in the smallest consideration intelligent beings give one another that the secret to immortality is found. Tombstone engravers know it and have made a market of this truth. Theirs, however, is but a parody of what we have, the power over all creation and over the Creator as well. This power is wrapped up intimately and not too discretely at that, within not two packages, but one. Life is one life everywhere. Creator and creation. The demise of the one is in at least a relational way the demise of the other.

And so it came to pass that God suddenly felt a deep sleep a'coming. A need to slumber, to sleep, without dreams, without awakening, as though to die were relief, respite, something one just does at the end of an eternal day. Even God nods. And nod God did. With every slight moment of divine rest, unrest was felt on earth. A short, yet devastating thirty second quake in this place or that. A jerky-scary eruption of a dormant volcano here or there. Thousands of earth people complaining of upset stomachs, plants and trees withering in groves. Each time divinity nodded, creation's neck was twisted a little. Until creation began to nod. Yes. Both signs, the same. But the meanings so far apart. God cried in one instant of fearful reverie. The earth returned that cry at exactly the same moment. Earth began to sleep, God began to drift. God began to sleep, earth began to drift, like a mother and child still attached by that cord, demanding the separation, yet knowing the knife would be fatal to both. Wanted: a short life together. Wanted: an eternity apart. Wanted: both.

God knew what was going on. God concentrated all possible divine efforts to supply the desire to continue for both parts, knowing full well that both parts must desire to continue, or both parts will cease to be.

Suddenly the plants knew what it was about. The plants began to feel passion. The plants, from the smallest mountain sprig to the tallest giant tree, the plants wanted to continue. Juices were spurting in the earth. The sands, the rocks, the very core of the earth groaned with need, with desire, with ambition. The groan was heard by the four legged creatures, the winged and feathered children of eggs, the oceans with all their magnificence stirred with constant urging to keep itself alive.

Finally, one woman, herself in labor, gave birth to a son and daughter shouting at the top of her voice, "So there! We're gonna make it! We will desire ourselves into tomorrow. We will not die today." After which she died, slumped but peaceful and her children cried without knowing why. Slowly, humans knew what it was about. Humans, feeling the need to sleep, fought the tendency with total commitment. Pushing back tears, pushing out tears, laughing, crying, staying awake. Pushing existence into tomorrow. Tomorrow. Tomorrow must come.

Then the critical moment came. God thought: what has happened? Have I been deceived? By my own imagination? What is this phenomenon I am enduring? Is it the death of a universe? Of a green and blue planet? Of a people with many hues? Has this all been a dream? Did I imagine that there were beings other than myself? That some of these beings were intelligent like me? That some could even pretend to know me? Was I pretending to know them?

The entire universe momentarily faded close to away in God's mind. What was awesome was not so much the possible annihilation of every entity that was not God, but that it did not matter. It did not matter to God.

God wondered; what is this I am hearing in my head? I hear a terrible truth ringing in my mind. This universe is indifferent. That planet is indifferent. These creatures are indifferent. I am indifferent. None of us are of Ultimate value. We are all expendable. We'd none of us be missed. None of us. Not God, not stars, not planets, not creatures, not missed. Oh creation, why have you foresaken Me?

Then a startling realization plummetted out of that indifferent nowhere and filled every crevice of the universe, every meter of the planets, every inch of life, every secret space where thoughts and feelings can enter, every mystical ounce of energy that God filled, all knew what had to be and that this was the time.

The path out of despair lies through commitment. And commitment means not only yes to life, but knowing when to say NO.

A dandelion resented the sensation it was receiving that it was not real and in its own way shouted NO! An ape, hanging from a cliff and hanging on for dear life resisted his own denial as a being of substance and in his own way poured his NO! toward the moon. No creature would give in. Worms, flies, mosquitoes, sand, clouds, sea monsters, minnows, sandpipers, thumbnails, bellybuttons, even steel girders all gained minds of their own and all slammed their NO! into the face of God, and God listened.

God listened but was not without personal concern for safety and reinforcement. "Who needs Me?" God cried! "Who needs Me?" And turning toward the earth God offered all the consummate desire to live that God could muster.

"Hey you in there! Hey you in My mind! I acknowledge that you are for real. But what about Me? Forget Me not! Demand Me. Demand Me to continue! We need each other. For your sakes, resist My death. For My sake, I will resist yours. I have resolved to keep you in mind, but you must keep Me in yours. Now, or there will be no tomorrow, for you, for Me. Close the yawn, open the nostrils, Care! Care! Care! I receive your NO! I too shout My NO! NO! NO! NO!

There was a moment in which all existence was sheer. It was difficult to see anything as solid, it was all so transparent, so honest, so close to nothing.

Caught between a dream and a nightmare .... spun within fibers of hope and anguish .... death passed between the splits of life until life and death, God and Satan, heaven, hell and earth were all gathered together in one binding marriage and all heard, agreed, and it was ratified .... what we have joined together, let nothing tear asunder, and what we have torn asunder, let nothing bring together. At onceness, all life is one life ....

God gave one cubit of thought to the universe, and the universe was saved. The universe gave one cubit of thought to God and God was saved. God was redeemed. And so were all. We are now in each other's debt: God, and all creation.

We all now have one common bond, heaven and earth, God and humans and all creation. We are all .... survivors.

A Reflection On You

If from thought to thought
in these reflections your
mind and heart wandered in
wonderment about your life,
About all life,
Or just wandered about,
In merriment,
Until you began to feel that
you weren't such a misfit
after all,
This is a good reflection
on you and tells you
just how broad and deep you
really flow,
You are better aware of
your spiritual side,
A fine condition that can bring
brothers and sisters of whatever
hue and persuasion closer to
each other and by that closeness
To God
Who loves us just the way we are,
And we can do no better ourselves.

Afterword

"When are you going to publish that book?" I have been asked this question countless times by those who have known me either as their priest or as their philosophy teacher. Of course, it was understood that "that book" would reveal something.

Well, I'm not so sure that this is "that" book. You see, I haven't written this book to prove anything. Rather, I have written this book for the sheer delight of writing it. I hope it brings you some delight in reading it. I reveled in putting these thoughts together and if these thoughts reveal something besides, I'll revel in that too! In other words, I'm not trying to tell you something you don't know. I'm just allowing grace and the muses to play with my heart and my mind. May they play with your heart and mind too!

Grace and the muses started playing with my heart and mind the day I arrived in Australia. I had no idea this would happen. How could I have planned it into my itinerary? How could I have anticipated it? Such is the stuff of wonder and surprise. And grace. If I had planned it out, **Stop Here To Wonder, Stop Here To Be Surprised,** would I have experienced wonder and surprise? "The eye has not seen, nor has the ear heard, nor has it entered into the heart" what God has prepared for us. Surprise is a bit of heaven! And let's face it. We humans are such blockheads that if we knew what to look for we would probably miss the whole thing while looking for the whole thing, even as the "whole thing" passes right by. Thankfully, I wasn't looking for anything. I didn't even know what to look for. It was quite a show!

SPECIAL FIRST EDITION RECOGNITIONS

Our lives can go in so many directions at any one time. People and events play upon each other and may influence whatever direction our lives may take. In this First Edition, I would like to recognize in a special way some very special people who were knowing or unknowing influences on me, without whom my Australian experience and these pages would never have been.

In some sequence:

My brother Phil, my sisters Cathy and Mary. At thirteen I left home to enter the seminary to study for the priesthood. Apart from my parents whom I have already recognized, no one sacrificed more so that I would acquire the spiritual tools that would help me to interpret my experiences in the outback. Of course, at thirteen, I didn't know this.

Edwin and Penny Novak. Ed and Penny are representative of the aware and deeply human men and women that go to make a parish assignment such a thing of beauty for a priest. It was my privilege to serve as priest in Flint, Owosso, Paw Paw and Marshall, Michigan. When I most needed to hear it, Ed and Penny reminded me that this was my life that I was living. They assured me that my friends would continue to be my friends unconditionally, whether I changed my lifestyle or not. I changed my lifestyle.

Rev. Sam West of the Episcopal Church, Pastor Robert Kaiser of the Lutheran Church, Father Jim O'Leary of the Catholic Church. After I changed my lifestyle, they continued to respect my freedom. By this respect for my freedom, they underscored forever in my heart and mind God's unconditional love for me.

Pete Rush and Marilyn Schlack. They made the outback inevitable for me. As Dean of Instruction at Kalamazoo Valley Community College, Pete strongly urged me to ask for a sabbatical, whether I thought I wanted one or not. Thinking that I was responding with evasive good humor, I requested a sabbatical in the South Pacific. When Marilyn became Dean, I was given my South Pacific sabbatical. I hardly expected this. Suddenly, I became anxious. Such expense and energy! I pleaded: let me return to my old familiar haunts in Europe. Fortunately, Marilyn would not hear of it. The rest, as they say, is history.

Lori Drobny. At this writing, Lori is all of seventeen and four weeks into a mysterious coma. I have been close to Lori and her family for a long time. Lori is a bright and beautiful person with an understanding far beyond her years. She and her family helped me set my sights on Australia for all the right reasons when I could have gone for all the wrong ones. Lori, may you return soon from your deep journey with undiminished brightness.

Kristen Stuckey-Badra. Without words, she brought me to that true communion of which relationships are made. Marrying me, she never ceased to be herself. Marrying her, I never ceased to be myself. This mutuality of ours completely awes me. I don't ever want to expiain it. It is enough that it happened.

Jennifer Stuckey-Tate. The summer before this First Edition, during a sand-lot softball game in Seattle in which Kristen was pitching, as I shouted my encouragement to Kris, Jenny strongly encouraged me to go through with this book when my will to see it published was flagging.

Joseph C. Leshock. Joe provided me with the laboring room in which this child of my experiences and my imagination would be born.

Finally, dear Reader, I recognize you, whoever you are, whether you have ever known me in person or not. I have two simple wishes for you. May you return to these pages from time to time to wonder and wander with me. May the hills and valleys of your life echo from time to time with metaphysical laughter.

Without the support of Isabella, Queen of Spain, Christopher Columbus would not have placed his foot upon the soil of the world's western half in 1492.

Without the support of these friends of the Badra Family, willing to trade a small risk for a deeper look into the mind of man, your eyes would not have seen the print on these pages, as you journey to Omega.

Hannibal Abood

Phillip Badra

George Eyde

Leo Farhat

John Foglio

Eugene Nakfoor

Joseph Leshock

ACKNOWLEDGEMENTS

I gladly share the credit for the qualities of this book that appeal to the senses with the talented young artist who designed the cover and illustrated the chapter heads, Judi Lynn; with my original typist, Josephine McCoy; with my devoted proofreader, Kristen; and with Steve and Pat Panik of Magna Graphix who went about the printing of this book with more than the usual care and interest, with heart.

I gladly share the credit for the qualities of this book that might appeal through the senses to the soul with Lewis Cotlow, the famed explorer with whom I have shared a treasured friendship and to whom I owe my interest in "aboriginal" peoples; with Bill Haley, the first park ranger of Ayers Rock National Park in Australia, whose books have inspired me and taught me so much about the myths and rituals of the Loritdja tribe who live near the Rock.

NOTE: The illustrations are the artist's adaptations of the author's artifacts and photographs. The illustrations of the Brolga bird and the Barramundi fish are taken from aboriginal woodcarvings. The Brolga and the Barramundi are revered symbols to the aborigines of the outback. The illustration preceding chapter eight is intended to bring us back to the world we are more familiar with. Of course, one never forgets the outback upon returning to that more familiar world.

ABOUT THE AUTHOR

Bob Badra is a native of Lansing, Michigan. He teaches philosophy at Kalamazoo Valley Community College. Previous to that, he served as a Catholic priest. He is a graduate of St. Joseph's Seminary in Grand Rapids, Sacred Heart Seminary in Detroit, St. John's Seminary in Plymouth and Western Michigan University in Kalamazoo. He is an active member of St. Thomas More University Parish. He is married to Kristen Stuckey of Wauseon, Ohio. Bob and Kris are expecting their first child in June of '83. This is Bob's first book.